Think Through
Geography 3

Mike Hillary
Julie Mickleburgh
Jeff Stanfield

Contents

Contents

1a Industry

• Alfreton: no longer a suitable location •

- What industries were here in the past?
- What industries are here now?
- Why has there been industrial change?
- What is the effect of factory closures?

B

1974 My first Job

On leaving school I got a job in a large engineering factory that made machinery for the engineering industry. I worked from 9am-5pm Monday to Friday and had four weeks' holiday a year. The factory was very modern, machines rather than people did a lot of the work. Most of the boys found jobs in the engineering works, concrete-moulding and metalwork companies. Wages were good because you had to have qualifications and skills. The girls worked in the knitwear factories, many complained because it was very noisy and hot on the shop floor. It was often said that it was easier to find work if you were young or a woman.

A

1965 Alfreton Mine, Granddad, Dad and Uncle Jack

Granddad Cottam worked down the mine for all of his working life, until it closed in 1968. After that he didn't work again, having to take early retirement due to poor health. Grandma Cottam became the main breadwinner as she continued to work in one of the many knitwear factories.

Uncle Jack was transferred to another pit and his whole family had to move. After that we didn't get to see much of them. Dad worked down the mine as an electrician. When he became redundant he got a place on a training course and found work with a local building company.

YOUR ENQUIRY

In this enquiry you will:
- identify different types of economic activity
- describe and explain Alfreton's changing economic structure.

In your enquiry you will have to look at Alfreton's future prospects and suggest how the area can continue to develop industrially.

C

1988 Helen showing off her typing skills

Although unemployment levels rose in the UK, there always seemed to be plenty of work around here. Smaller purpose-built industrial estates were built in the 1980s and this is my daughter Helen working in the office of a local haulage company. These smaller companies employed fewer workers and their jobs seemed less secure. The jobs created required fewer skills and therefore paid less.

D

1995 Jackie working in a factory retail outlet

I was made redundant in the early 1990s and couldn't find work. Gone are the days when a job is for life, unlike Granddad's time. There seem to be fewer factories making things and more factory outlets and shopping centres selling things. There are more distribution, warehousing and service type jobs, such as DIY centres, fast food outlets and hotels. The jobs created today seem to be mainly for younger people, those who are less skilled and for older females. The pay is low and the hours long.

E

Factory closure, 2001

The town is buzzing with the news that many of the knitwear factories are going to close. Hundreds of people are at risk of losing their jobs. What are people going to do in the future? I'm glad I'm getting old now.

Step 1

Look at the photographs and copy and complete the table to show how the employment structure of Alfreton has changed over time.

Type of job	Sex	Average age	Skills / education	Pay	Working conditions
Miner	M	35	None	Good	Very poor. Long shifts. Dirty, hot conditions. Dangerous, risk of explosions/rock falls.

From coal to coats

A   Pre 1969

Alfreton's industrial growth was founded on local deposits of iron ore and coal. The **colliery** opened in 1839 and became the main employer for the area until it closed in 1968. The cheap supply of resources attracted other industries, such as ironworks, but they only employed men. Women were not employed in large numbers until after 1945 when the **textile industry** developed in the town. By the time the pit closed in the late 1960s, equal numbers of males and females were employed in the main industries of the town.

A coal pit

STEP 2

1 Draw a pie chart graph to show Alfreton's employment structure, using the following figures: manufacturing 50%, service 28%, other 22%.
2 a Produce a timeline to show how the industrial structure of Alfreton changed from the late 1960s to 2001.
  b Add these comments made by local people to your timeline.
    Miner: 'There are plenty of jobs for women but few for school leavers and men.'
    Local Councillor: 'Our new economy will be based on a variety of industries, our eggs won't be in the one basket of the coal industry.'
    Shopkeeper: 'A large supermarket in the centre of town will either destroy the high street or add more vibrance to the town.'

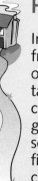

Homework

Interview your family and family friends and find out what types of jobs they do. Complete a table like that on page 5. If you can, find out what jobs your grandparents did and produce a separate table. Compare your findings with those of your classmates. Compile your results. Produce a graph to show the types of jobs that people do and how they have changed over time. Describe and give reasons for the differences you can see.

E

DIY centres, supermarkets and fast food outlets have been built on the old factory land. The town is also planning to twin with Blackstone Valley in the USA and hopes to develop its tourist trade. But these industries need fewer workers than the factories and those they employ tend to be young, unskilled and paid low wages. Not all business proposals are successful – a large supermarket wished to locate near to the town centre, but the plans have been rejected and they have been forced to look at a **brownfield** site.

New McDonald's drive-through built on the former Jaeger site

B

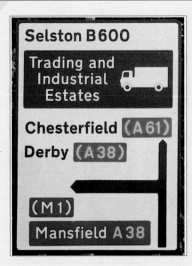

Selston B600
Trading and Industrial Estates
Chesterfield (A61)
Derby (A38)
(M1)
Mansfield A38

Excellent access

1969–1980

The mine closure led to a rise in male unemployment levels. In 1969, the Government decided to help the area out by giving firms money to relocate there, and other incentives were offered such as lower rates and taxes. The road system was also improved, for example the A38 was built to link up to the newly-opened M1. Old mining land was cleared and redeveloped. New large factories were built. Manufacturing, rather than mining, became the main source of work. Still only a few larger industries dominated, including textiles, chemical production, concrete and stoneware production, and engineering.

C

1980s industrial units

1980s–1990s

In the 1980s, smaller industrial units were built on industrial estates. These housed double-glazing firms, car dealerships and car repairs companies. Small-scale specialist manufacturers of springs, boxes and jigsaws were attracted to the area. By 1982 the Government had stopped its financial aid to the area and larger companies went elsewhere.

D

Arthur Glenn Park Factory Outlet next to J28 M1

1990s–2000

Some of the larger textile factories have already closed. However, other factories have increased their income by setting up factory retail outlets to sell their clothes direct to the public. Originally factory shops were located within the factory building but today many have purpose-built shops away from the factory site.

Factory closures – here we go again

More textile gloom looms

Devastated, massive blow for workers

Hundreds of jobs to be axed

Heartbreak for textile industry

A The worst fears of workers at Alfreton's under threat knitwear factory came true this week as Coats Viyella announced its closure, resulting in the loss of 438 jobs. The likelihood of re-employment in the industry is bleak. Many people have worked there for years, often with other family members.

All the textiles manufacturing has gone abroad to countries like Morocco, China and Turkey and the customers cannot do anything about it.

Coats Viyella is a global company that has a number of knitwear factories in the local area. It made clothes for companies like Marks and Spencer, and Jaeger. The company was forced to close factories because its profits fell by £8.5 million in a single year. This was because shops like Marks and Spencer demanded that the manufacturers lowered their prices. When they refused, they ended their contracts and went to foreign companies to buy their goods. Coats Viyella has now stopped making clothing and home furnishing and is going to concentrate on the production of threads.

Adapted from the *Chad* (Alfreton's local paper)

STEP 3

1 Why are the knitwear factories threatened with closure?
2 How would closing the textile factories down affect the town? Make a list of the effects this would have.

The following points might help you.
• foreign competition makes prices cheaper
• derelict land can be redeveloped
• people move away to find work.
3 Show these effects in a flow diagram.

THINKING THROUGH YOUR ENQUIRY

'How should Alfreton develop?'

You work for Amber Valley District Council. You have been asked to produce a briefing document for the Minister of Trade before a decision is made about how the area should be developed in the future.

Using the resources in this chapter you should be able to:
- Give a brief history of the economic development of this area.
- Identify the economic strengthens and weaknesses of this area.
- Decide whether this area should continue with large-scale manufacturing or move towards up-market/specialised production. Give reasons for your decision.

+	–
Strengths	**W**eakness
Opportunities	**T**hreats

The following writing frame may help you structure your report. Remember to use all the resources in this unit.

1 Give a brief history of the economic development of this area.
2 Identify the economic strengths and weaknesses of the area. To help you, make a copy of the table above and put the labels below in the correct box.
   Labels: skilled and qualified workers; companies are flexible and respond to changes in demand; very good access via motorway network; close to Derby and Nottingham; very creative designers; global reputation; close links with dye and thread manufacturers; too many designers; overseas competition; cannot compete in terms of prices; lack of investment (money needed to buy new machinery); reputation for quality; exports goods around the world; using the Internet to sell goods; setting up design rather than manufacturing companies; imports; loss of tariffs; high cost of equipment; lack of business skills; local links with art colleges has improved the skills of local designers; chemical industry is designing new technical materials; growth of service industries.
3 Now look at the photographs and resources in the chapter and add any additional ideas you may have.

1b Industry

• The fashion for changing industrial locations •

- Where is the textile industry located today?

- Why is its distribution changing?

- What are the effects of this change?

- Why is the UK no longer a suitable location?

A derelict mill with windows smashed

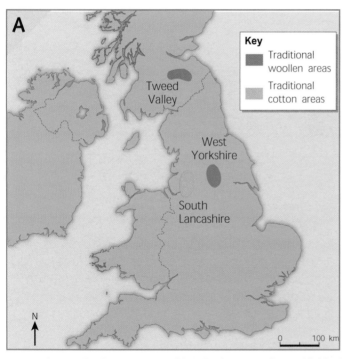

Location of the UK textile industry (pre 1960s)

Key

Traditional woollen areas

Traditional cotton areas

The UK has had a long tradition of textile and clothes manufacturing – at the turn of the century it was the country's largest employer and exporter, however its importance has declined over the past 40 years. By 2001, it was the eighth largest manufacturer, producing £17 billion worth of goods and employing 279,000 people. Since 1994, UK output has fallen and 1,300 clothing companies and 469 textile firms have shut down.

Textile companies in the UK have become increasingly uncompetitive, as they have been unable to match the lower prices charged by companies based in less economically developed countries (LEDCs), e.g. India, Taiwan, Korea and China. In these countries wage levels are much lower, e.g. in China the average wage rate can be as low as 15p an hour. These companies do not have to invest large sums of money in buying machinery because they can just employ more workers instead! They also benefit from not having to offer their workers contracts, minimum wages, holiday pay, pensions or sick pay – as a result, working conditions are often very poor.

• drawing a map •

YOUR ENQUIRY

In this enquiry you will:

- examine the geographical distribution of the textile and fashion industry
- identify why its location has changed.

At the end of the enquiry you will produce a board game which will examine the causes and effects of the relocation and globalisation of the textile industry.

To protect the British textile industry, **tariffs** had been imposed (taxes which are added to imported goods, to make them more expensive) so that British goods remained cheaper and consumers continued to buy them. However, the World Trade Organisation has achieved international agreement to remove all tariffs by 2005. This will add further problems to the UK textile and clothing industry.

Step 1

1 Look at map **A**. Copy it onto an outline map and shade in the traditional woollen and cotton producing areas.

2 Look at the table below. Using the information, add labels onto your map to show the areas where textile and clothing manufacturing is concentrated today.

Cotton	North-west, e.g. Bolton
Fine knitwear (e.g. Cashmere)	Scotland, e.g. Scottish Borders Selkirk/ Galashiels
Linen	N. Ireland, e.g. Newtonards County Down
Woollens	Yorkshire, e.g. Huddersfield
Knitwear	East Midlands, e.g. Alfreton
Footwear	e.g. Northampton
Clothing	North and East London Birmingham Leicester Manchester

3 Produce a spider diagram to explain why the UK textile industry is finding it difficult to compete with companies that are located in LEDCs.

4 Produce a pie chart to show the structure of the UK textile industry, using the following figures: clothing 43%, technical materials 21%, medical materials 10%, protective clothing 2%, others 24%.

Homework

Make a collage or cut out photographs from magazines to show the types of materials and fibres used in clothing. Make a list of the types of materials and fibres used and whether they are natural or synthetic. Compare this to those used in the past.

Where in the world do your clothes come from?

A

B

Clothes shop in the UK

Clothes shop in an LEDC

Globalisation describes the process whereby individuals, groups, companies and countries become increasingly interconnected. It is due to improvements in technology and telecommunications, which have made the world seem a smaller place.

Globalisation has been encouraged by the growth of transnational companies locating factories across the world. The creation of manufacturing jobs in LEDCs has led to improvements in living standards there, increasing the demand for luxury items and creating new markets, which in turn has attracted more manufacturers to locate there. Globalisation has been criticised for diluting national differences and creating a single global culture.

STEP 2

1 What does the term 'globalisation' mean?
2 Explain what the phrase 'the world is getting smaller' means. Give examples from your own life that shows this.
3 Do you think that the development of a single global culture is a good or a bad thing?

Homework

1 Clothing is a basic need. Think about the number of items you have in your wardrobe. Choose your favourite clothes and look at their labels (often found along a seam). Copy and complete the table below.

Type of clothing	Shop bought from	Brand/ company	Fibre made from	Place of manufacture
Sweatshirt	GAP	GAP	Cotton	Sri Lanka

2 Compare your results with your friends' results and add their findings to your table. (See the Longman web site.)
3 Locate where each product has been produced by marking them on an outline map. Identify the designer/company by using different symbols.
4 Describe the distribution of clothing manufacturing shown.

Fashion victims

Sweatshop conditions in an LEDC textile factory

D

I work for a company which makes clothes for a large transnational corporation which has a famous brand name. I haven't had a day's rest in weeks. I work from 8 am to 9 pm. We are not paid overtime. If there is an important order then we are made to work until it is finished. If we say 'no' then we are sacked. If we have any food we eat while we are working. We are paid by the amount we produce.

A young person in a sweatshop

Working conditions in a Victorian textile factory

F

Women and girls over 14 years are employed for 12 hours a day and 8 hours on a Saturday in most textile factories. The workrooms are often overcrowded, dirty, ill-ventilated and insufficiently heated. Younger girls are illegally employed and it is not surprising that they look tired; but there are always plenty of other girls to take their place, so they keep on going.

Victorian factory inspector

 • analysing photographs • • interrogate a datebase •

G 1.3 thousand million people worldwide have to live on less than 70p a day. One reason why globalisation has failed to help the poor is because the poor receive less benefit from economic growth. Unfair trade deals between rich companies and poor countries, who need the contracts, mean that the workers are often exploited. They work long hours, in bad conditions, for very little money. Many poorer countries also have to compete with other LEDCs and therefore have to offer even lower wages, e.g. in places such as Indonesia textile workers earn 57p for a ten hour day.

CAFOD report

Not all LEDC countries are benefiting from the shift in the location of the textile industry. Pakistan was one of the first LEDCs to develop a modern and effective textile industry. However, it is now also facing competition from other countries such as India and China. Textile products including raw cotton, yarns and fabrics make up 65% of Pakistan's exports. A lot of money has been invested in new machinery from Japan which is in continual use, but Pakistan still finds it difficult to compete, as wage levels and electricity costs are even lower elsewhere.

H

The Chinese Ashan cotton and dyeing factory based in the Liaoninh Province is now building a clothing factory in Morocco. The goods made here will be sold in the African market. All the processing machinery will be imported from Japan and the Republic of Korea.

BBC web report

Extension

There are many international organisations which campaign against sweatshop conditions and child labour. (See the Longman web site.)

1 What kinds of changes/action do they want to see happen?
2 Who are they trying to get involved in their campaigns?
3 Do you think they will be successful? (Give reasons to explain your answer.)

STEP 3

1 Look at photograph **C** and describe the working conditions of some people in LEDC factories.
2 Compare the working conditions of a UK Victorian textile factory and an Asian factory today in sources **C** to **G**. Look at the type (age/sex) of people working there. Why do you think these people are employed?
3 Explain why some LEDCs will not benefit from the global shift of the textile industry. (Think about countries like Pakistan). What effect will this shift have on them?

Small tailor's shop in Thailand

Not all clothing manufacturing in LEDCs is by large-scale transnational companies. Many small-scale businesses are important. In the northern city of Chang Mai, Thailand there are over ninety textile factories as well as hundreds of small tailor shops (see photograph **A**).

The shop owner is not Thai, but Nepalese. He left Nepal when he was younger and was looking for work. He had family who were already living in Thailand, so he came and stayed with them. Over time he learnt to become a master cutter and tailor and set up business with his uncle. Eventually he saved enough money to buy his own shop. His younger brother has also migrated from Nepal and works for him. The shop is open seven days a week from 10 am to 12 pm.

The brothers are able to speak a number of languages, including English, Thai, German, French and Swedish – the main languages of the people who visit the city. Once the design and materials are chosen, a price is agreed and measurements are taken.

A typical tailor's shop in Thailand

The garment can be made within a matter of hours. A silk suit (including trousers, waistcoat, jacket and extra set of trousers) hand-finished costs between £80 to £100.

Using a mobile phone, the shop owner summons an **outworker** who is available to do the job. The outworkers are often migrants who are new to the country and are desperate for work. They often work illegally and are therefore cheap to employ. The outworkers work for themselves, usually in family groups. They have to provide their own sewing machines, threads and tools and are only paid for what they produce. If they have no orders then they make no money (**piece rate**). They will work for a number of different tailors at any one time.

The faster they work, the more they can produce. They will arrive in minutes, usually by moped to beat the traffic. Instructions and material are handed over, and within a few hours they are back with the pattern cut out and tacked together. The garment is fitted and altered. A finished suit can take less than 12 hours to make.

Even a small tailor's shop in Thailand will have an Internet website and address. (See the Longman web site.) Once measurements have been taken they are kept, and orders can be placed via the Internet.

B

Fitting a suit

STEP 4

1 Look at the flow diagram. Draw your own flow diagram using the following labels in the correct order:
  - the pieces are tacked together
  - the finished product takes between six hours and a few days
  - pattern is drawn and cut – a skilled job
  - outworker gets to the shop quickly – time costs money
  - price agreed and material chosen
  - the suit is fitted and changes made
  - measurements are taken.

2 Make a list of the inputs into the system shown by your flow diagram.

3 What are the advantages to the owner of employing outworkers?

4 What are the disadvantages of being an outworker?

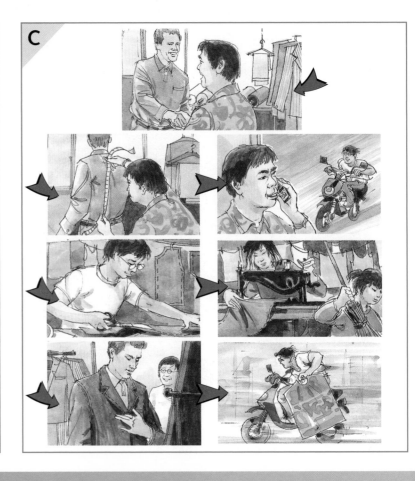

C

THINKING THROUGH YOUR ENQUIRY

56 HOME 55 54 53 52 51

44 45 47 48 49

42 41 37 36

29 30 34 35

28 27 23 22

15 16 20 21

14 13 12 11 10 8

START 1 3 4 5 6 7

'Globalisation game'

Design a board game, which you can play with between four and six people, that shows the effects that 'globalisation' is having upon the world's economy and the textile industry.

To help design your game:

1 List the advantages and disadvantages of globalisation.
2 Identify groups of people who are affected positively and negatively by globalisation.
3 List the countries which are winners and those which are losers.
4 Identify how the textile industry has changed over time.
5 Think about how you will know who has won your game.
6 Think about a set of rules.
7 Design the board/counters/cards.
8 Think of an imaginative name for your game.

• designing a board game •

1c Industry

• You reap what you sow! •

- How does the production of natural fibres harm the environment?

- How does the production of artificial or synthetic fibres affect the environment?

All materials are made from either artificial or natural fibres.

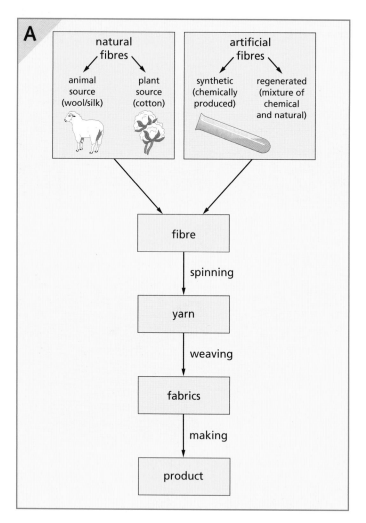

The production of fibres and the processes used to produce textiles and clothes can have a number of harmful effects on the environment. Look at table **B**.

B **Environmental problems related to the textile industry**

1 Over use of water supplies for irrigation of crops.

2 Use of pesticides and toxic chemicals to increase yields.

3 Reducing bio diversity; planting large areas with a single crop, i.e. cotton.

4 Water pollution from chemical plants.

5 Production of greenhouse gases when producing artificial fibres.

From *Business,* 2nd October 2000

Many fabrics today are now made with artificial fibres. These are made from oil-based chemicals. The processes used produce large quantities of carbon dioxide, which is a greenhouse gas. This may be causing **global warming**.

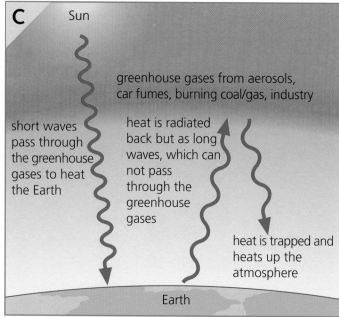

The greenhouse effect

 • understanding a diagram •

D

carbon dioxide and other gases released

risk of explosion, therefore away from settlements

produces unpleasant smells and smoke

the air is warmed

large areas of cheap flat land required

near to coast, so that oil tankers can dock

A petrochemical plant

Artificial fibres are produced in petrochemical plants. It is cheaper to locate a petrochemical plant next to an oil refinery, where the crude oil is processed.

STEP 1

1 Make a copy of table **B**. Add on a second column to explain why each one is a problem.

2 What is a synthetic fibre made of?

3 What does the term 'global warming' mean? Why is it happening?

4 Where are petrochemical plants located?

5 How can the processes in petrochemical plants cause environmental damage?

Homework

Many resources can be recycled as a way of using them more efficiently and reduce environmental damage. Either, design a poster to explain why resources should be recycled; or, find out what types of products can be recycled and produce a local map showing the recycling points.

YOUR ENQUIRY

In this enquiry you will:
- find out how the production of the raw materials used in the textile industry can damage the environment.

In your final enquiry you will have to produce an article explaining how the environment has been harmed because of our demand for textiles.

Quenching the white gold's thirst

A

Key
- Mountains
- International borders

0 | 1000 km

Arctic Ocean

Russia

Caspian Sea

Aral Sea

Kazakhstan

Uzbekistan

Turkmenistan

Iran

Mongolia

China

Japan

N

The location of the Aral Sea

B

A ship in the middle of the dry Aral Sea

In 1960, the Aral Sea was the fourth largest inland lake in the world. It covered an area of 66,458 km^2, but by 1996 it had shrunk to 28,800 km^2. Its volume of water has decreased by 80% and the average sea level has fallen by 17 m, at a rate of up to 90 cm a year. This has increased the water's salt content; it is now five times saltier than before.

C

'I walked up a dune to a beach and looked out to sea, but it was 100 km away. The ships lie in their dry beds, at anchor for ever.'
'It's the worst ecological disaster in the world. The water and fish have gone, the soil and air are poisoned and the people have been left to choke to death in the dust.'

A.A. Gill

D

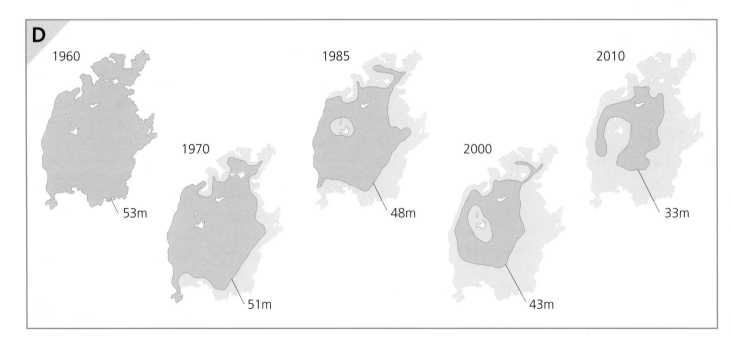

1960

1970

53m

51m

1985

48m

2000

43m

2010

33m

A series of outlines to show the disappearing Aral Sea

From A. Goudie, *The Human Impact on the Natural Environment*, Blackwell 1986

 • drawing a sketch map/annotate •

STEP 2

1 Draw a sketch map to show the location of the Aral Sea.

2 Mark on the outline of the sea's boundary in 1960 and 1996.

3 Read the information in the text on page 20 carefully. Add labels to your sketch map to show how the sea has changed over time.

STEP 3

1 Why did the farmers need so much water?

2 Why did the farmers describe cotton as 'white gold'?

3 Why did dangerous chemicals have to be used here?

The region around the Aral Sea is an important farming area. It produces cotton for the textile industry. Cotton is a cash crop and the locals call it 'white gold'. It is a thirsty crop and needs a lot of water to grow. Because the region's climate is hot and dry, the crop has had to be artificially watered or irrigated. The main source of water came from the Amudar'ya and Syrdar'ya rivers, which flow into the Aral Sea. Millions of litres of water were taken from these rivers and pumped onto the land. Often the water was wasted and evaporated away before reaching the plants. The problems were made worse by the fact that fertilisers and chemicals were also used in large quantities. Some of the chemicals were so dangerous that they had been banned by many countries (e.g. DDT) but were still used here.

Cotton pickers in the Aral Sea area

The impacts caused by the reduction in the sea level

Climate

The climate of the area has changed. Summers have become drier and shorter and winters longer and colder. Strong winds blow over the dried out soil, creating dust and salt storms. Over 200,000 tonnes of salt and sand are carried by the wind each day and spread over a 300 km area.

The Aral Sea

The plants and animals

As the Aral Sea became saltier and warmer the number of species of fish fell from 20 to 5. The number of mammal species reduced from 70 to 30 and the number of bird species from 319 to 168.

The soils and water supply

The soils and water supply have been heavily contaminated by the fertilisers and pesticides which were used. There is now a lack of fresh drinking water. In some places water is brought in by tanker, or people drink the water from the irrigation canals.

Health and living conditions

There has been an increase in diseases such as tuberculosis, liver and kidney disease and cancer.

STEP 4

Look at the resources and write two paragraphs to explain how the drying up of the Aral Sea has affected the environment and people.

Our people are dying like flies. Over one million people living in the country are suffering from the effects of chemical pollution.

Russian doctor

We have high levels of heavy metals, salts and other toxic substances in our drinking water, and the bulk of our vegetables are contaminated with pesticides, such as DDT which is still used here in great quantities.

Russian doctor

Economic changes

The Aral Sea has lost its fishery and shipping industries completely. Thousands of people have lost their jobs and have been forced to leave the area. The population has declined from 82,900 to 72,500 people within the past ten years.

Solving the Aral Sea's problems

Since the 1980s, the cultivation of new large irrigated areas was banned and large-scale water resources projects have been introduced. At the same time, measures to improve living conditions have been adopted.

Irrigation method

THINKING THROUGH YOUR ENQUIRY

'Aral Sea presentation'

Imagine you are a scientist who has visited the Aral Sea and is speaking at an international conference. Produce a Powerpoint presentation that will accompany your talk.

Suggested structure:
- locate the area (see Step 2)
- explain what has happened to the Aral Sea since 1960 (see Step 2)
- explain why this has happened (see Step 3)
- identify the environmental and social effects of this reduction in the sea's water level (see Step 4)
- explain why this is an important global issue that we should all be concerned about.

2a Population
• Home sweet home? •

- Where do most people live?
- What makes people live in some areas and not in others?
- How is the pattern of population changing?

A

Population = people
The study of population is called **demography**.

I like living here. It's so quiet and peaceful

A sparsely populated rural area in a Scottish island

Some areas of the United Kingdom (UK) have large numbers of people living in them. Other areas have very few people living in them. Why do people choose to live in some areas and not in others?

One of the most important things to many people is where they work. Many people like to live close to the place they work in. This means that the most densely populated areas are often in towns and cities, where there are lots of jobs.

I like living here. It's close to work and the shops.

A densely populated urban area in London

The Hebrides Scottish Islands

London

0   150 km

• photograph interpretation • geographical vocabulary •

YOUR ENQUIRY

In this enquiry you will:

- describe and explain the terms population density and population distribution
- explain why some areas are densely populated and some areas are sparsely populated
- describe and explain the population distribution in the United Kingdom.

At the end of the enquiry you will write an account to describe and explain the distribution of population in Europe.

People everywhere

STEP 1

1 Do you live in an urban or rural area?
2 Would you describe your local area as densely or sparsely populated?
3 Which areas within your local area are densely populated or sparsely populated?
4 Look at photograph **C** and Map **D**. Why do you think there are so few people living in the Scottish Highlands and Islands?
5 Explain what geographers mean by the term 'population density'.
6 Where would you like to live in the future?

Homework

Find out how far two people you know travel to work.

Collect your findings as a class and draw graphs to show how far people travel to work in your local area. Name two advantages of living close to where you work and two advantages of commuting to work. Which would you prefer to do? (Consider time, pollution, noise, cost of housing, leisure activities.)

E We measure the **density** of population by the number of people living in a square kilometre.

$$\text{DENSITY} = \frac{\text{POPULATION}}{\text{AREA}}$$

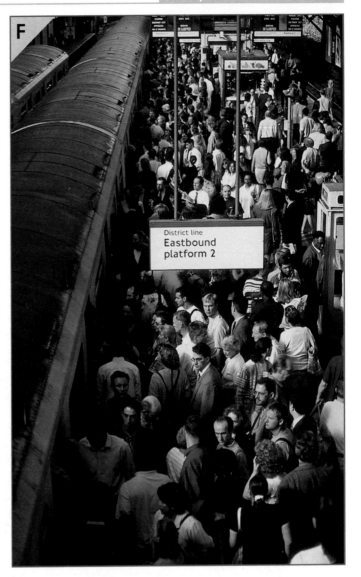

F

Commuters arriving at a crowded London railway station

Today, in the UK over 80% of people live in **urban** areas. Only 20% live in the relatively sparsely populated countryside or **rural** areas.

Not all people want to live near where they work. Some people travel long distances to work. We call these people **commuters**. Some commuters travel over 100 miles a day to and from work to cities like London in the UK. Commuters often choose to live in the countryside because they feel they can have a better quality of life away from a large town or city. Many people in the UK now choose to live within commuting distance of a large city like London.

Pattern of people in the UK

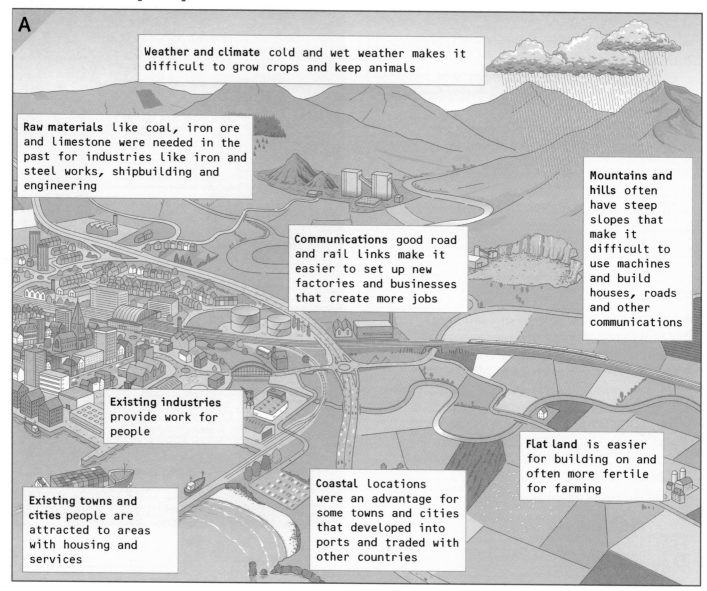

A

Weather and climate cold and wet weather makes it difficult to grow crops and keep animals

Raw materials like coal, iron ore and limestone were needed in the past for industries like iron and steel works, shipbuilding and engineering

Mountains and hills often have steep slopes that make it difficult to use machines and build houses, roads and other communications

Communications good road and rail links make it easier to set up new factories and businesses that create more jobs

Existing industries provide work for people

Flat land is easier for building on and often more fertile for farming

Existing towns and cities people are attracted to areas with housing and services

Coastal locations were an advantage for some towns and cities that developed into ports and traded with other countries

Factors affecting population density

In the past, before the industrial revolution, most people in Britain lived in the countryside (rural) areas where they could farm the land and provide their own food. People needed good farmland, a good water supply and an area that was not too cold or wet. People were spread out much more evenly across the country, often living in small villages about five miles apart.

During the industrial revolution, large numbers of people moved to work in the new factories in the towns and cities. Coal was needed to power the new factories, so many of these towns grew on coalfields in the Midlands and northern England.

In the UK there are both densely populated areas and sparsely populated areas. By understanding the reasons why people live in some areas and not others, we can explain the pattern of population density. Many factors affect a person's decision about where to live. The different types of jobs people do are an example of a **human** factor, connected with people. Climate is an example of a **physical** factor, something natural.

 • explaining a pattern •

STEP 2

1 Sort the factors in diagram **A** into physical factors and human factors.
2 Using an atlas, match the conurbations listed A to G with the numbers on map **B**.
3 Using an atlas, on an outline map shade and name three areas which are densely populated (over 150 people per square kilometre), and three areas which are sparsely populated (under 10 people per square kilometre).
4 Sort the factors in source **C** into two groups: for London and for the Scottish Islands.

Extension

Describe and explain the pattern of population density in map **B**.

C

Factors affecting population density and distribution

- The region has very cold winters, cool summers and high rainfall.
- It is a centre for communications and trade.
- The mountainous landscape and very steep slopes makes it difficult to build roads and railways.
- Communications are poor and the region is remote from the main centres of population and industry.
- It is the capital and major centre for industry and commerce.
- Very poor, thin, and infertile soils make farming very difficult.
- There are a wide range of jobs in the service sector, e.g. offices, shops, transport and entertainment.

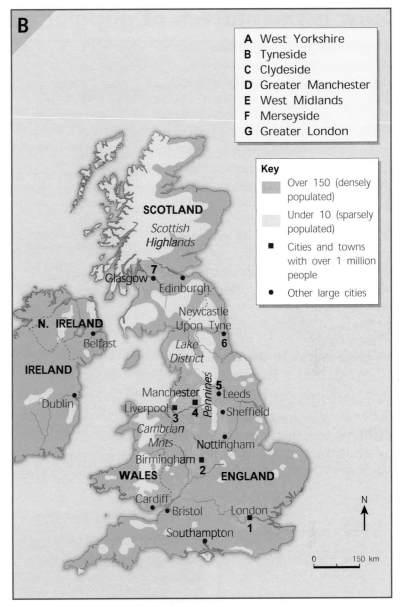

B

A West Yorkshire
B Tyneside
C Clydeside
D Greater Manchester
E West Midlands
F Merseyside
G Greater London

Key

▨ Over 150 (densely populated)

▨ Under 10 (sparsely populated)

■ Cities and towns with over 1 million people

● Other large cities

Population density in the British Isles

The Scottish Islands and Highlands are areas of low population density. There are very few jobs available, and because of these harsh physical factors and **economic** problems, few people live here.

Greater London is an area of very high population density. Human factors play a large part in explaining why this is one of the most densely populated areas in England.

In the past many people moved away from the Scottish Islands and today some people are moving out of London – the population distribution is constantly changing.

How is the pattern of population changing?

People are moving to new homes in rural areas because of the problems in **inner city** areas. These **greenfield** sites are areas of farmland and countryside that have not been used for housing in the past. Many people are against these new houses being built on this land (see Book 1: Unit 2c). Land is becoming a scarce resource in the UK as increasing numbers of people seek a new home. The government is trying to recycle some of the existing land in cities, which has been used for factories and housing in the past. These **brownfield sites** might be the answer to the land shortage in the future.

Schemes like the Docklands scheme and the area around the Millennium Dome in London are an examples of areas that have been or will be redeveloped.

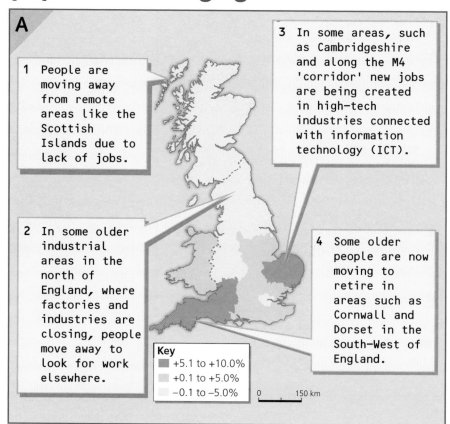

A

1 People are moving away from remote areas like the Scottish Islands due to lack of jobs.

2 In some older industrial areas in the north of England, where factories and industries are closing, people move away to look for work elsewhere.

3 In some areas, such as Cambridgeshire and along the M4 'corridor' new jobs are being created in high-tech industries connected with information technology (ICT).

4 Some older people are now moving to retire in areas such as Cornwall and Dorset in the South-West of England.

Key
+5.1 to +10.0%
+0.1 to +5.0%
−0.1 to −5.0%

0   150 km

Population change 1981–1991

STEP 3

1 Look at the area around the Millennium Dome in photo **B**. What do you think should be built on a site like this?

2 Why might some people protest at the building of new housing on greenfield sites?

3 Look at map **A**. Using the places labelled and the key, briefly describe the changing pattern of population in the UK.

B

New housing area around the Millennium Dome

 • explain changes in a geographical pattern •

THINKING THROUGH YOUR ENQUIRY

'Patterns of people in Europe'

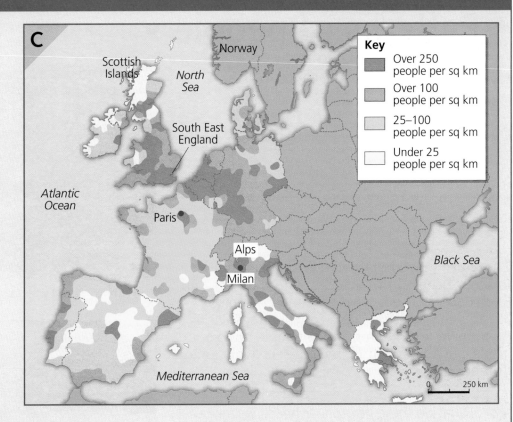

Density of population in Europe

Your task is to describe and explain the population density and distribution across Europe.

You will need: atlas maps (political [country names], geology, relief, climate, economic) and all the information and questions you have answered in this unit.

You should:

- describe the pattern of distribution: name areas of high and low population densities
- explain the pattern of distribution: give reasons for the high and low population densities.

Use the following guide to help you.

1 **Title:** The pattern of population density in Europe

2 **Subtitle:** Areas with high population density
Some areas such as _____, _____ and _____ are densely populated with over 250 people per square kilometre.

3 **Subtitle:** Areas with low population density
Some areas, such as _____, _____ and _____ are sparsely populated with less than 25 people per square kilometre. (Step 2)

4 **Reasons for population distribution**
Areas with high population density, such as _____ are areas with...
Areas with low population density, such as _____ are areas with...

5 **Conclusion**
The distribution of population in Europe is very even/uneven because ...
I think the main reasons for the population distribution are _____, _____ and _____. In the future the population density might change as more people _____. (Step 3)

2b Population
• Patterns of people •

- How many people are there in the world?

- How is the pattern of population changing?

- How many more people will there be in the future?

There are over six billion (six thousand million) people in the world. Where do they all live? Look at the figures in table **E** on page 31. You can see that some continents, such as Asia, have a large number of people and some areas, such as Oceania, have a relatively small number of people.

A What do these newspaper headlines mean?

> ## Population pressure – can the Earth cope?

> ### Family planning – a success story?

> ## Average family size set to fall to 1.2 children in some countries – happy families?

> ### 'When I'm 64' – can we afford the pensions?

> ### 'She's leaving home' – village set to become a ghost town?

> We think a large family is a good idea.

The Khan family – a large family in Pakistan

> The government would like us to have a small family.

The Tang family – a small family in China

YOUR ENQUIRY

In this enquiry you will:
- describe the patterns of population by continent
- investigate the changes in population over time
- understand why some countries are trying to control their population increase.

At the end of the enquiry you will write a report on an international youth conference called to discuss the future of the world's population, called: 'Population – problems and possibilities'.

Global distribution of population

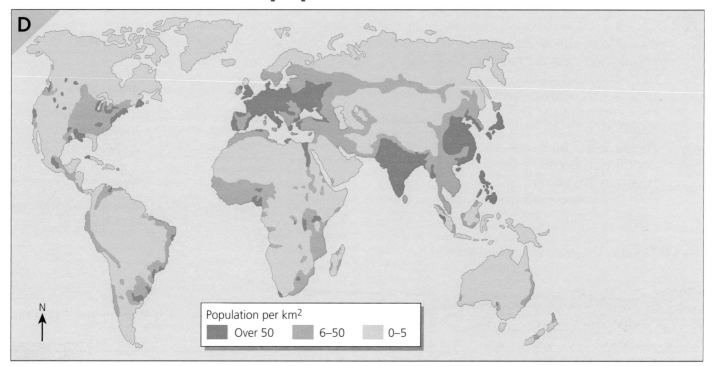

D

Population per km²
- Over 50
- 6–50
- 0–5

N

E

Population total (by continent)			
Continent	Total population in millions	Infant mortality rate	GNP per capita US $
Africa	771(572)	88	660
North America	303(266)	7	28,130
Latin America and the Caribbean	512(414)	35	3,950
Asia	3,637(2,866)	56	2,450
Europe	728(493)	9	13,890
Oceania	30(25)	29	15,630
World	**6,000+**	**57**	**5,170**

Key

Infant mortality rate: number of children who die before the age of one, per 1000 of the population

GNP per capita (US$): average amount of wealth per person, per year in US dollars

Oceania: Australia, New Zealand and the Pacific Islands

(572): 1986 figure

Population Concern
©Population Reference Bureau 1999

STEP 1

Look at table **E**.

1 Which continent has the most people?
2 Which continent has the fewest people?
3 Rank the continents in order of total population.
4 Draw a bar graph or a pie chart to show the total population for each continent. You could use a computer spreadsheet to draw the graphs.
5 Which graph is most effective in showing world population: a bar graph or a pie chart?
6 Look at map **D**. Describe the pattern of world population density (see Unit 2a).

Extension

Rank the continents in order of infant mortality rates and GNP. Draw a line to divide them into two groups based on these figures.

Homework

Research up-to-date figures for the continental areas on the Longman web site. How have they changed?

Growth of the world's population

A

The rise in the world's population was very gradual until the start of the nineteenth century and then rose very rapidly. The population in an area may rise or fall. The rise in the population is called the **natural increase**.

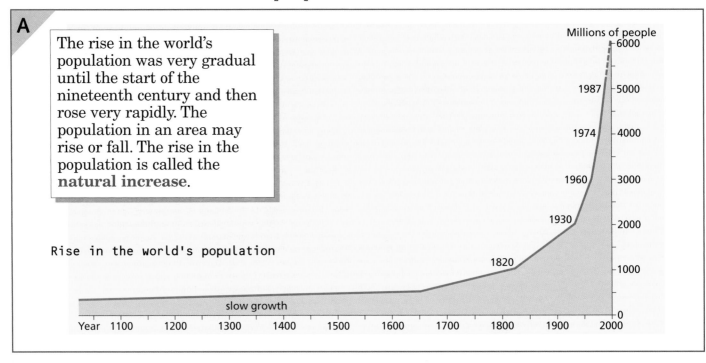

Rise in the world's population

slow growth

B

Continent	Birth rate per 1000	Death rate per 1000	Growth rate per 1000	Natural increase annual %	Doubling time in years
Birth rates and death rates around the world					
Africa	39	14	25	2.5	28
North America	14	8		0.6	119
Latin America and the Caribbean	24	6		1.8	38
Asia	23	8		1.5	46
Europe	10	11		-0.1	never!
Oceania	18	7		1.1	64
More developed world	11	10		0.1	583
Less developed world	26	9		1.7	40

C

Natural increase = birth rate – death rate
BR – DR = NI

The **birth rate** is the number of live births per 1000 people per year.

The **death rate** is the number of deaths per 1000 people per year.

STEP 2

1 Complete the figures for growth rates, e.g. Africa 39 – 14 = 25
2 Draw a bar graph to show the birth rates and death rates for each continent. Use the same column for birth rates and death rates.
3 Describe the pattern of birth rates and death rates shown by your graph.

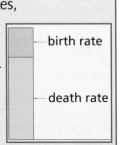

 • data handling •

China – one child policy

D

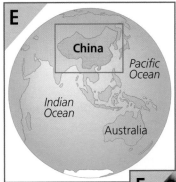

China's population growth 'slowing'

China has announced that its first nationwide census in a decade puts the Chinese population at 1,260,000,000, including people living on the island of Taiwan – over one and a quarter billion people! The figure means that the population has grown by 132.2 million people since 1990, an increase of 11.7%, said Zhu Zhixin, Director-General of the National Bureau of Statistics. Annual growth was 1.07%, down 0.4% from the rate in the 1980s. Mr Zhu said the census showed that China's compulsory birth-control policies were effective in holding down population growth.

But some experts believe the latest figures underestimate the population growth. Since the late 1970s China has restricted urban couples and many rural families to just one child to reduce the strain on food production and other resources. But BBC Beijing correspondent Rupert Wingfield-Hayes says that serious questions remain over the accuracy of the figures. Counting China's massive population is extremely difficult, made only more so by its 'one child' policy, as tens of millions of people with extra children are thought to have hidden them from the census takers for fear of being punished. The total figure was substantially lower than independent estimates, which put the number of Chinese as high as 1.5 billion.

The census results also confirm fears that China's gender imbalance is growing at an alarming rate. There are now 117 boys born in China for every 100 girls – way above the international norm of 106 boys for every 100 girls. China's age-old preference for boys is being made worse, both by the one child policy and by modern technology, which can detect the sex of a child early in pregnancy. This technology has led to an increase in abortions when parents know the foetus is a female.

BBC News, 28th March 2001 and UK Census (BBC News, 3rd April 2001)

STEP 3

1 What was China's official population estimated to be in 2001?
2 How many more people are there since 1990?
3 How does this compare to the total population in the UK of around 60 million?
4 Why might the real figure in China be even higher?
5 How much has the rate of population increase in China slowed since the 1980s?
6 What problems have the one child policy caused?

E

China

Pacific Ocean

Indian Ocean

Australia

F

Chinese family

How do populations change over time?

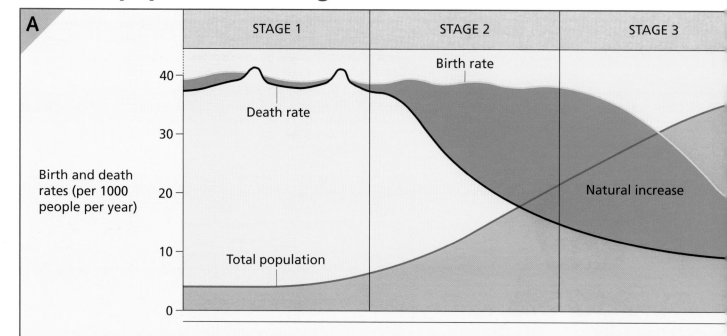

A

STAGE 1	STAGE 2	STAGE 3

Birth and death rates (per 1000 people per year)

Death rate

Birth rate

Natural increase

Total population

In stage 1 people have large numbers of children (a high birth rate) but many of them die young and many people die before they reach old age (a high death rate). Occasionally, during periods of war, plague or famine the death rate might rise above the birth rate and there would be a *fall* in total population. This can still happen in some parts of the world today, such as the native people in the Brazilian rainforest.

In stage 2 the birth rate remains high, but the death rate begins to fall rapidly due to improved hygiene, sanitation and medicine. The total population increases *rapidly*. The growth rate is high, between 2% and 4% per year. Some countries in Asia, Western Africa and Central America are still in this stage.

In stage 3 the birth rate begins to fall due to improved family planning and changing social and economic conditions, e.g. pensions for older people, cost of children. Countries such as Argentina, China and Jamaica are in this stage.

A country like the UK (United Kingdom) has taken 150 years to go through this demographic transition. The UK was in stage 1 before 1750. At this time there were agricultural and industrial revolutions which increased food supply and created better living conditions, which meant that more people survived. Stage 2 lasted from 1760 to around 1880. In stage 3 people started to have smaller families for economic and social reasons – the birth rate fell dramatically from 1880 to 1940. Stage 4 lasted from 1940 until the present day. The UK may enter stage 5 soon if birth rates fall below death rates.

STAGE 4	STAGE 5

Natural decrease

→ Time

In **stage 4** the birth rate has fallen to a figure just above or the same as the death rate. Japan and most countries in Western Europe have reached this stage. The natural increase is very small.

In **stage 5** people continue to have fewer children and the birth rate falls below the death rate. In this situation there is a natural *decrease* in population. Germany and Sweden and some countries in Eastern Europe already have a *negative* natural increase.

Diagram A shows how birth rates, death rates and total population change over time. This change in population over time is called the **demographic transition** (demographic = population, transition = gradual change).

The demographic transition

STEP 3

1 Look at diagram **A** on this page showing the demographic transition. Copy and complete the table by choosing from the following words:

high   low   falling   rising

2

Stage	Birth rate	Death rate
1	High	
2		Falling
3	Falling	
4		Low
5		Low

3 What is the natural increase in each of the stages: small or large?

4 During which two stages does the total population rise very rapidly?

5 Look at diagram **A**. In the table you have completed for question 2, add approximate figures for the birth rates and death rates, e.g. over 40 per 1000 or under 15 per 1000.

Extension

Look at the following figures for birth rates and death rates. Copy and complete the table with the correct stage of the demographic cycle (figures are for 1999).

Country	Birth rate (per 1,000 of population)	Death rate (per 1,000 of population)	Stage?
Japan	10	7	4
Italy	9	10	
Gambia	43	19	
India	28	9	
United Kingdom (UK)	12	10	

Population structure

The change in birth rate and death rate affects not only the total population but also the **population structure**. The population structure refers to the percentage or number of males and females in the different age groups. The total population is divided up into age groups 0–4, 5–9 and so on up to 85+.

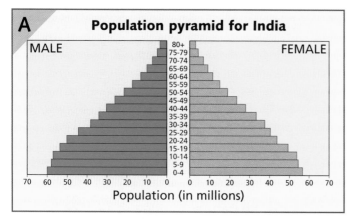

From U.S. Census Bureau, International Data Base

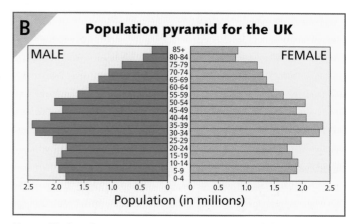

From U.S. Census Bureau, International Data Base

In the past most countries had a population pyramid shape like the one for India in diagram **A**. This pyramid is typical of a LEDC (less economically developing country) with a large percentage of young children and young people. The pyramid narrows quite quickly due to the high **infant mortality rate** (the number of children who die in their first year) and the large numbers of children who die due to illness and poor diet. The top of the pyramid is narrow due to the relatively low **life expectancy** (the average age a person can expect to live in that country). Low life expectancy is again typical of LEDCs.

If we go back in time, the UK's population pyramid would have looked like this, but as the birth rate and death rates have changed so the population structure has changed. If we look at diagram **B**, the 'pyramid' now looks very different. Now in MEDCs (more economically developing countries) the birth rate has fallen and people are having smaller families and fewer children than in the past. At the other end of the age structure far more people are living to a 'ripe old age' and people

are expecting to live beyond their 'three score and ten' (which was the old saying referring to the typical life expectancy of 70 years). Average life expectancy in the UK is now 77 years of age (men 74, women 80).

By studying the population pyramids, you can see not only the effects of changing birth rates and death rates but also predict what might happen in the future. This is what governments have to do in order to plan for the number of schools and hospitals and to care for the elderly. Population pyramids are divided into three groups: young dependants, the economically active and elderly dependants. We can compare the population structure of two countries by referring to these groups.

STEP 4

1 Look at diagrams **A** and **B**. Compare the two population pyramids for India and the UK. Use three sub headings: young dependants (under 15), economically active (16–64 years of age) and elderly dependants (65+).

• population structure •

THINKING THROUGH YOUR ENQUIRY

'Population – problems and possibilities?'

Imagine you are attending a United Nations youth conference to discuss the issues connected with the changes in population: birth rates, increase in population, changing structure of population and migration. You are a youth parliament representative from a country. Choose one of the following countries: MEDC (United Kingdom, Italy, Australia, Japan, or USA) or LEDC (Kenya, India, China, Brazil, or Mexico).

The title of the conference is **'Population – problems and possibilities?'**

There are a number of **key questions** to be discussed:

- Should we try to control world population increase before it is too late?
- Should we try to keep a global balance of population between continents?
- Should governments try and influence population growth and structure?

The illustrations in source **C** may help you.

1 Choose **one** of the key questions above you wish to discuss as a group.
2 You will need to research the question using this textbook, other reference books, newspapers and electronic sources of information (Internet).
3 In the role of a country's representative, you will then be able to offer your government's view on one of these questions. Make your own notes or presentation for the debate. For example, you may be able to offer just information in the form of statistics about your country, or give advice from your country's experience of the issue.
4 You might like to offer suggestions or help in trying to improve the situation – what could your country do to try and improve the situation?
5 Having debated the issue, you might like to make one or two general suggestions that can be agreed on by a majority of countries.
6 You might also vote whether you agree or not with the statements/questions.

Extension

1 As well as giving your country's views, you might also be able to give examples of these issues from other parts of the world.
2 What other questions or issues about population might you be able to research and answer?

C

Is there a problem with the world's population or not? Are there too many people or not?

The population is constantly changing. **Birth rates** have been falling over the last 50 years.

As people get richer and better educated they tend to want smaller families.

Birth control is now more widely available.

Death rates now are lower than they have ever been. Improved medical care, better food and sanitation are just some of the reasons why the death rate has fallen.

The rise in population may start to slow down all over the world as the standard of living improves for people and they want smaller families.

Eventually the world's total population may stop rising and simply stay the same as people only have enough children to replace themselves.

2c Population
• Population and resources •

Not just a question of numbers!

- Is there enough space for all the people in the world?

- Are there enough resources?

- Can the Earth support six billion people?

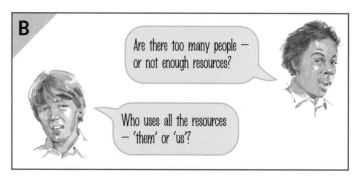

B

Are there too many people — or not enough resources?

Who uses all the resources — 'them' or 'us'?

A

Wealthy people in Bombay India

C

Eco-friendly, sustainable community in Wales

Every single person needs water, food and a home to live in. We all would like some clothes to wear, water to wash in and somewhere to sleep. These are what we would regard in the 'rich world' as the basics. For millions of people around the world, these are still luxuries. Every person uses some of the Earth's resources everyday – some people more than others.

YOUR ENQUIRY

In this enquiry you will:

- describe the link between people (population) and resources
- understand the terms 'overpopulation' and 'underpopulation'
- investigate some of the issues involving population and resources.

At the end of the enquiry you will take part in a debate to try and answer the question, 'Can the Earth cope with the world's population?'

• photograph interpretation • global citizenship •

Everyone counts!

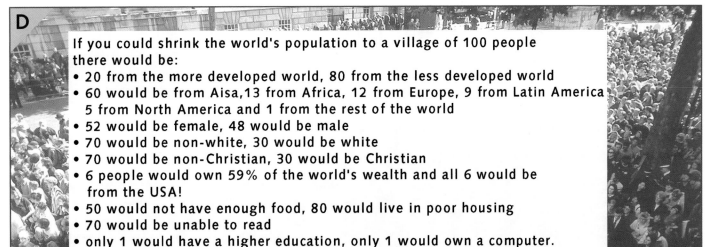

D

If you could shrink the world's population to a village of 100 people there would be:

- 20 from the more developed world, 80 from the less developed world
- 60 would be from Aisa,13 from Africa, 12 from Europe, 9 from Latin America, 5 from North America and 1 from the rest of the world
- 52 would be female, 48 would be male
- 70 would be non-white, 30 would be white
- 70 would be non-Christian, 30 would be Christian
- 6 people would own 59% of the world's wealth and all 6 would be from the USA!
- 50 would not have enough food, 80 would live in poor housing
- 70 would be unable to read
- only 1 would have a higher education, only 1 would own a computer.

A message e-mailed to the author as part of Friendship Week 2001

STEP 1

1 What are the basic resources that all people need? Make a list of five.
2 'All the rich people in the world live in rich countries.' True or false?
3 In the past someone once said, 'Just think, one day every town might have a telephone.' Why does this sound quite funny to us today, but is still true in some parts of the world?
4 20% of the world's population consume 80% of the world's resources. Do you think this is fair? Give two reasons why you think this has happened.
5 How has a rise in population and standards of living affected our use of resources?

Homework

1 What are the essentials that people need to live?
2 If you had to give up five things you take for granted, what would they be?
3 If you could only have ten things on a desert island, what would they be?

Furniture, televisions, telephones, electricity and cars are taken for granted by most people in the more economically developed countries (MEDCs) and rich people in the less economically developed countries (LEDCs).

As people become richer they tend to buy more goods, which in turn uses up more resources. One rich person will tend to use far more of the Earth's resources than ten poorer people. As the population of the world increases so more resources are being used up. Some of these are **non-renewable** and will eventually run out.

E

People sleeping rough in the UK

Australia – not enough people?

Many children who live in some parts of Australia have to listen to the radio and use the post for their school lessons. If they are ill they call the 'flying doctor' service. This service covers two-thirds of Australia. Doctors operate from bases equipped with radio. They fly out to distant cattle ranches, sheep stations and settlements if there is a medical emergency.

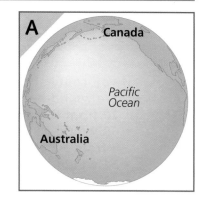

A

B

Some parts of the world are very **sparsely** populated. Australia is the world's most sparsely populated continent. Australia's total population is 19 million, but it covers 7,686,848 million square kilometres. If density equals population divided by area, the average **population density** is only 2.5 people per square kilometre. The **population distribution** is also very uneven.

Flying doctor visiting isolated farmstead

Why are there so few people living in some parts of Australia?

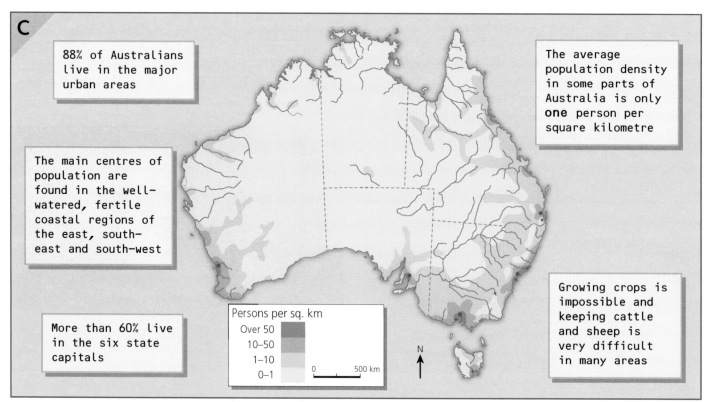

C

88% of Australians live in the major urban areas

The average population density in some parts of Australia is only **one** person per square kilometre

The main centres of population are found in the well-watered, fertile coastal regions of the east, south-east and south-west

More than 60% live in the six state capitals

Growing crops is impossible and keeping cattle and sheep is very difficult in many areas

Persons per sq. km
Over 50
10–50
1–10
0–1

0   500 km

N

Choropleth map showing population density in Australia

 • population density •

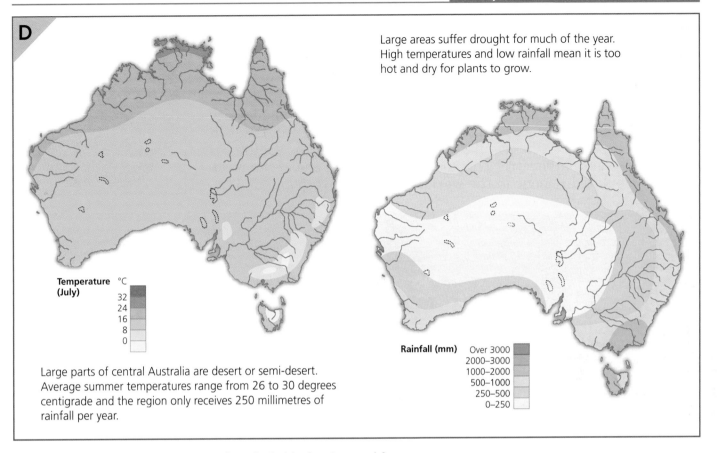

Large areas suffer drought for much of the year. High temperatures and low rainfall mean it is too hot and dry for plants to grow.

Temperature °C
(July)
32
24
16
8
0

Large parts of central Australia are desert or semi-desert. Average summer temperatures range from 26 to 30 degrees centigrade and the region only receives 250 millimetres of rainfall per year.

Rainfall (mm)
Over 3000
2000–3000
1000–2000
500–1000
250–500
0–250

Maps showing temperatures and rainfall in Australia

Countries like Australia and Canada have very low population densities and many areas contain very few people. Many parts of northern Canada are covered in snow and ice for much of the year. Those areas in northern Canada that are not covered in snow and ice often have a very rugged landscape, very poor soils and very few roads. Despite all this it is estimated that Canada, which at present has a population of 31 million, could support a population of 50 million. Canada is a rich country. The population is rising only very slowly. The average wealth of people is the same as the UK. It is rich in raw materials and resources. Canada and Australia are both examples of countries, which could be said to be **underpopulated**.

Northern Canada – a sparsely populated area

STEP 2

1 Using an atlas, name four cities in Australia
2 Look at Map **C**. Where do most people live in Australia?
3 Why do so few people live in central parts of Australia?
4 Using the maps **C** and **D**, describe and explain the overall 'pattern' of population distribution in Australia.
5 Why are countries like Australia and Canada said to be 'underpopulated'?

 • choropleth map reading • comparing patterns •

Too many people?

Some parts of the world might be said to have too many people, compared with the resources available. We would call this **overpopulated**.

Look at photograph **B** of Hong Kong. The average population density is 5,351 people per square kilometre (13,874 per square mile). But in some parts of the city the population density is as high as 25,400 people per square kilometre! This makes Hong Kong one of the most densely populated regions in the world. But it is it overpopulated?

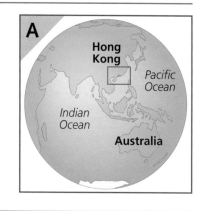

Hong Kong

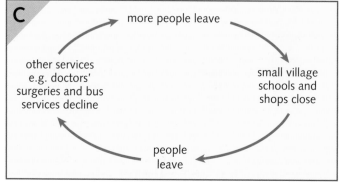

Process of rural depopulation

Migration in the UK

Whilst many places may have too many people, some places in the United Kingdom may not have enough people. Some rural areas are suffering from a lack of people. As people move away from small villages to look for work there are fewer people left. This process is called **rural depopulation** (see source **C**). Villages in parts of Scotland, Wales, Northern Ireland and rural England could probably support more people if there were more jobs and services. Over time this process means that some parts of the UK are underpopulated!

Small remote village with shops closing

STEP 3

1 Imagine how big a square kilometre is. Look on an Ordnance Survey map and see how much is covered by the school grounds. Now imagine over 25,000 people living in that square kilometre in Hong Kong.

2 Look at photograph **B**. How can so many people live in such a small area?

3 Imagine you are leaving a small rural village to go and live in a city. Write a letter to a friend or relative explaining why you are leaving.

4 Look at the 'Fact or opinion file' in source **F** opposite. Which do you think are facts and which are opinions?

E

How can we balance population and resources?

There are several ways we could balance the world's population and resources.

Either:

1 We stop using so many resources (in which case standards of living might fall).
2 We try and stop the rise in population, and even begin to reduce the population in some areas (but this would mean preventing people having as many children).
3 We begin to change the way we live, consume less, use renewable sources of energy and raw materials, and recycle more of what we use already (not everyone might want to do that).
4 We find new resources, invent new forms of power and use the resources more effectively (but still consume resources).

F

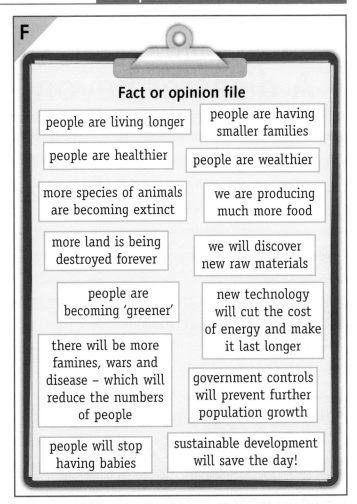

Fact or opinion file

people are living longer

people are having smaller families

people are healthier

people are wealthier

more species of animals are becoming extinct

we are producing much more food

more land is being destroyed forever

we will discover new raw materials

people are becoming 'greener'

new technology will cut the cost of energy and make it last longer

there will be more famines, wars and disease – which will reduce the numbers of people

government controls will prevent further population growth

people will stop having babies

sustainable development will save the day!

THINKING THROUGH YOUR ENQUIRY

'Can the Earth cope with the world's population?'

As part of a television or Internet web conference two people are debating this question.

One is a pessimist (someone who tends to think things will get worse) and the other is an optimist (someone who thinks things will get better).

1 Choose to be an optimist or pessimist. Prepare a short presentation about how things will get worse or how things might improve (Step 1 may help).
2 Using examples, explain how some areas are overpopulated, if you are the pessimist, and how some areas are underpopulated, if you are the optimist (Step 2).

3 Briefly explain either:
   • the problems and how they might get worse, if you are the pessimist, **or**
   • the solutions to the problems and how things will improve, if you are the optimist. (You might choose from the 'Fact or opinion file' – see Step 3.)
5 Now debate the question: 'Can the Earth cope with the world's population?' in front of the class or group. At the end you could vote as a group on whether the answer to the question is yes, no, or maybe.

 • literacy • fact and opinion • research for a debate •

3a Tectonic processes
• A disaster beyond comprehension •

- Why did an earthquake strike northern India in 2001?

- What impact did it have on the area?

- How can people help one another when disasters such as earthquakes hit?

A 'Heritage of centuries destroyed in minutes by Indian earthquake.'

Rahul Bedi

B

Afghanistan
China
Iran
Pakistan
Nepal
Indian Ocean
Oman
India
Bangladesh
20°
Arabian Sea
Bay of Bengal
Indian Ocean
0   500 km
Sri Lanka
10° N

Central Anjar after 2001 quake

Atomic bomb damage at the end of World War 2 in Japan (Hiroshima)

Note: The quake hitting India was 30,000 times more powerful than the bomb hitting Hiroshima

YOUR ENQUIRY

In this enquiry you will:
- investigate why an enormous earthquake struck northern India in 2001
- unravel the primary and secondary effects of the quake and examine how people attempt to support areas like this.

At the end of this enquiry you have to decide what you would include in an international, earthquake disaster, rapid-response centre.

 • investigating photographs and diagrams •

Why us, why northern India?

Friday January 26th 2001, 8.46am

The position deep inside the Earth's crust where the earthquake originates is known as the **focus**. The place on the earth's surface directly above this is the **epicentre**. The epicentre of the January 2001 Indian earthquake was near Bhuj and Ahmedabad in the north-west state of Gujarat (source **G**). **Shock waves** radiate out from these points (source **E**). These are what cause the massive destruction witnessed in the region, and in other places like California.

'It was like being on a swing as buildings shook violently, developed cracks and collapsed,' said one witness, Vinay Kumar in Ahmedabad. Quite often after the main quake has struck, **aftershocks** occur for long periods. These can hinder rescue work and cause still further damage. The main quake lasted for just over 45 seconds and registered 7.9 on the Richter Scale.

Seismologists recorded nearly 200 aftershocks in the following 24 hours, including one of a magnitude of 5.5, which in itself is quite large.

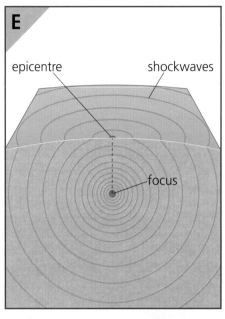

Points of an earthquake

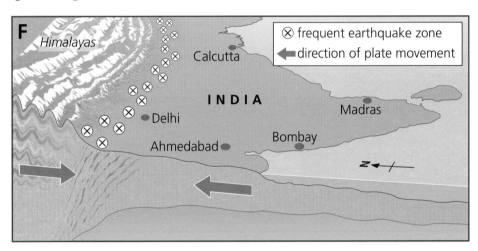

Plates in northern India moving together

Map of earthquake area showing key areas affected

STEP 1

1 Study photos **C** and **D** carefully. What do they show about the power of the Indian earthquake?

2 Working in pairs, write down key words which you would use to describe the scene after the earthquake struck (share your words with your partner). Select the best terms and use them to produce a short description of 'Anjar after the earthquake'.

3 Using sources **E** and **F** to help you, describe why northern India is an area of the world that is likely to suffer from earthquake activity.

4 Where was the epicentre of the January 2001 earthquake? Although most damage was close to this, what other points of the Indian sub-continent felt the impact of the earthquake (look at source **G** which shows the shock waves)?

From active communities to rubble

The earthquake which struck north-west India in January 2001, turned some thriving communities to rubble in seconds. Many people were at home preparing to celebrate Republic Day, a national holiday. Its effects were felt across India, Pakistan, Nepal, and Bangladesh. For example, in Bombay high rise buildings swayed and shuddered, lifts trembled and beds shook.

A

'To travel across the earthquake belt by helicopter, as I have done today, conveys the size of the catastrophic damage which has befallen India. Towns like Anjar and Bhachau have simply crumbled away, and the city of Bhuj is in irreparable ruins. Countless thousands of dead lie buried in the rubble, tens of thousands are homeless.'

W.F. Deedes, visitor with Unicef

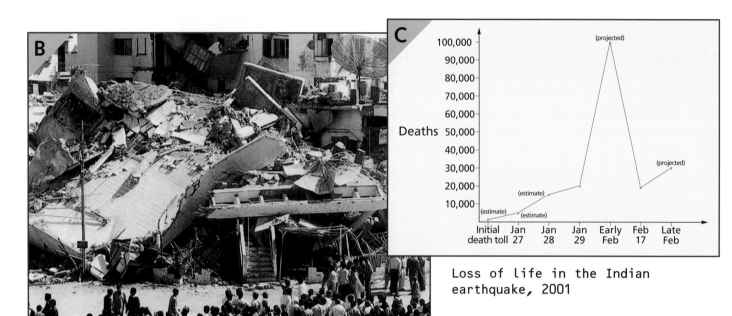

Loss of life in the Indian earthquake, 2001

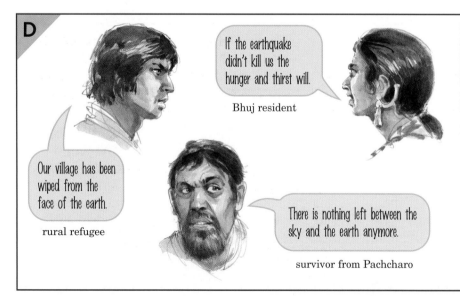

Earthquake damage in Ahmedabad

D

If the earthquake didn't kill us the hunger and thirst will.

Bhuj resident

Our village has been wiped from the face of the earth.

rural refugee

There is nothing left between the sky and the earth anymore.

survivor from Pachcharo

Within an 80 mile radius of Bhuj up to 100 villages have been wiped from the face of the earth.

Pachcharo a town of 40,000 near Bhuj was reported to be just a mass of concrete and mangled iron.

Press release

'The noise of the constant buzz of diggers, cranes and pneumatic drills drowned the cries of mothers waiting in vain for the rescue of their children.'

45 seconds that will remain with us forever

Disasters, such as earthquakes and hurricanes (see Book 1 page 58), have an immediate or **primary impact**. This impact may only last a few seconds, such as the 45 seconds of earth trembling that caused the chaos in north-west India. However, the affect on people and places after such a disaster (**secondary impacts**), such as rebuilding, often lasts for many years.

In Ahmedabad, 37 school pupils went back to school on Republic Day for an extra science class. They were buried alive when the earthquake caused their school building to collapse (primary impact). Later six were dragged out of the building alive, while rescuers fought to save others. The school will be rebuilt (secondary impact) like other buildings at a later date.

Rescue workers releasing victim: Champaben Seth, 90, survived because her head was protected by a large metal sewing machine

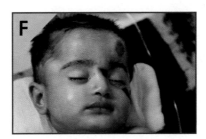

Murtza Ali survived because his dead mother's body protected him

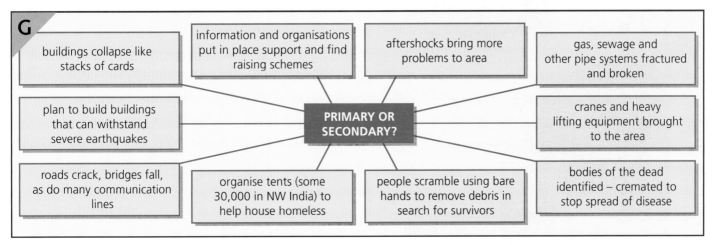

G

- buildings collapse like stacks of cards
- information and organisations put in place support and find raising schemes
- aftershocks bring more problems to area
- gas, sewage and other pipe systems fractured and broken
- plan to build buildings that can withstand severe earthquakes
- **PRIMARY OR SECONDARY?**
- cranes and heavy lifting equipment brought to the area
- roads crack, bridges fall, as do many communication lines
- organise tents (some 30,000 in NW India) to help house homeless
- people scramble using bare hands to remove debris in search for survivors
- bodies of the dead identified – cremated to stop spread of disease

STEP 2

1 Flown to Ahmedabad in devastated NW India, you are asked by your radio company to prepare a short tape of your findings. What radio 'images' would you send back to the UK about the impact of the earthquake? Use the sources on these twp pages to help you create your radio message.

2 Graph **C** shows the estimated death toll in the earthquake. Use bullet points to record what you think the graph tells us about the loss of life in this earthquake.

3 Why does the graph go up and down during January and February?

Homework

Look at the spider diagram in source **G**. Use it to help you to create a table showing primary and secondary impacts of the earthquakes. You can add your own points to the list.

Extension

'Some areas of the world (such as California) seem to be better prepared for coping with disasters such as earthquakes.'

Do you agree or disagree with this statement? (Don't forget to back up your viewpoint with evidence.)

Help is at hand

When disasters strike, people often forget personal and political differences, and support one another. As the world awoke to the news of the devastation of India, offers of aid poured in from around the world. This included support from India's close neighbour Pakistan. Long running differences between the two countries were put to one side. The need was for help and saving of lives.

A

INDIA EARTHQUAKE

In 30 seconds an estimated 25,000 people died in Gujarat, India.

Whole communities have been destroyed. Families devastated. Entire areas flattened.

Those who survive lack the basic needs: medicine, food and clothing. But worse could follow with fatal diseases. Mission India, a Christian organisation, is already there providing Family Survival Packs through our local partners. But we need many more.

£60 provides a whole Family Survival Pack, but any gift you can afford will help.

What happens in the next 30 seconds is up to you.

Please fill in this coupon or call now.

Photo: Reuters/Jason Reed

Yes, I want help families in Gujarat.

☐ £60 ← *Cost of 1 Family Survival Pack.*
☐ £40 ☐ £20 ☐ Other £_____
☐ I enclose a cheque made payable to Mission India or please debit my Access/Visa/Delta/CAF/MasterCard (circle one)

Card No. ☐☐☐☐☐☐☐☐☐☐☐☐☐☐☐☐☐☐☐
Expiry Date ☐☐☐☐ Valid from ☐☐☐☐
Signature_____ Date_____
Name Mr/Mrs/Miss/Ms_____
Address_____
_____
_____ Postcode_____

MISSION India

Registered Charity No. 1076598. MI64-3075 G

Mission India: India Earthquake Appeal Vedic Society Temple/Daily Echo Appeal

Types of aid

Aid comes in many different forms for example:

- money to help purchase items needed within devastated areas

- medical supplies to support work of doctors and nurses

- expertise – to help with rebuilding/redevelopment of hit areas

- blankets – for the hospitals and those people sleeping outdoors

- heat-seeking equipment/especially-trained dogs – to locate earthquake survivors.

Aid also comes from different sources.

- **Multi-lateral aid**: the 'international community' may provide support for areas that are affected by major disasters. For example, search forces from many different countries converged on NW India to help to release people from damaged buildings.

- **Bi-lateral aid**: one country may provide aid to another. For example, aid given by the former Soviet Union to Cuba or the USA to Central American countries. Some people think this type of aid is politically motivated (for the gain of the country providing the aid).

- **Aid organisations/private donations**: organisations may provide aid, such as Mission India or collections through disaster funds (see source **A** and also Oxfam's website).

  • citizenship • interdependence • interculturalism •

Connections

Although January 26th 2001 will be long remembered by people living in and around the state of Gujarat, its impact was worldwide, especially amongst the Indian communities with family connections in the region (see Source **B**). In Southampton UK the four Gurdwara temples and the Vedic Society temple, in conjunction with the local evening paper, organised round the clock collections of items such as blankets and clothes as well as cash. This was typical of many communities in the United Kingdom and other countries in providing personal donations and support.

STEP 3

1 Look at the list of types of aid on page 48 that can be given to areas affected by disasters such as earthquakes. Suggest another five items that would help people in these areas.
2 Source **A** shows an advert seeking donations for earthquake victims. Design your own hard-hitting poster for a national newspaper that would encourage people to help the disaster victims.

Extension

Using your library/information centre to help you, research one of the major aid organisations such as Oxfam. Describe a project that they are presently involved in worldwide.

B

Quake Doc is Mourned

Dr Ashok Nathwani specialised in childhood immunology and vaccination and childhood surveillance. He had been employed by Portsmouth Health Care NHS Trust since October 1995 and worked with children and families in Gosport as well as special needs children across the Portsmouth area. He died after being trapped when a building collapsed in the city of Ahmedabad. The doctor had gone to India with his father to scatter his mother's ashes as well as to attend a medical conference in Agra.

From *Southern Daily Echo,* 29th January 2001

THINKING THROUGH YOUR ENQUIRY

'It's your decision'

Now that you have investigated the causes and effects of earthquakes, you will be aware that many areas of the world require specialised help and support when disaster strikes. Work in groups to draw up a list of items that you would store in a large, international, earthquake disaster, rapid-response centre. The centre would respond immediately to the needs of devastated areas.

The list has been started for you. It notes the items to be stored and, most importantly, the reasons why they are to be included:

- tents to provide shelter for homeless peoples
- pneumatic drills for help with search and repair work
- heavy lifting cranes for the removal of earthquake debris.

3b Tectonic processes
• Rattling, rolling and shaking •

- What evidence is there to show that Earth is a very active place?

- Why do earthquakes and volcanic eruptions occur?

- What are earthquakes and volcanoes like?

- Why do these tectonic processes occur?

Our Earth is an extremely active place. Volcanic eruptions and earthquakes happen on a daily basis and are often not reported by the media unless they are enormous, such as the Indian earthquake of 2001. Most take place in certain areas (belts) of the world (see page 53). This is not always the case, however, with sizeable earthquakes affecting the British Isles (such as one measuring 3.8 in Cornwall in November 1996). Earthquakes and vulcanicity are examples of tectonic activity.

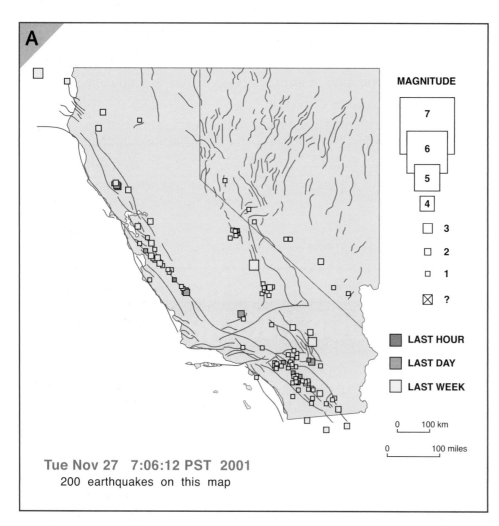

A

MAGNITUDE

7
6
5
4
☐ 3
☐ 2
☐ 1
☒ ?

■ LAST HOUR
■ LAST DAY
☐ LAST WEEK

0   100 km

0   100 miles

Tue Nov 27 7:06:12 PST 2001
  200 earthquakes on this map

Earthquakes within California, U.S.A.

From Northern California USGS (See Longman web site)

YOUR ENQUIRY

In this enquiry you will:
- investigate the nature, causes and effects of tectonic processes/ activity
- investigate the character of different plate boundaries, and the link between them and earthquake/ volcanic activity
- begin to investigate how people respond to these dynamic processes.

At the end of the enquiry you will be asked to write a short report entitled 'Active Earth', for a new booklet for Key Stage 3 pupils. You will need to give information about tectonic activity and where this most often occurs.

Why California?

There are many benefits of living in California. It has a Mediterranean climate and a range of job opportunities, for example in fast growing, hi-tech industries. It has become one of the richest regions in the world. However, the state has the misfortune of being situated where the North American plate and Pacific plate meet (see source **B**). These slide past each other in the region, along major **fault lines** such as the San Andreas Fault (see photo **C**).

As the North American plate slides southwards, it rubs against the Pacific plate moving northwards. Because of the colossal

Long view of the San Andreas Fault

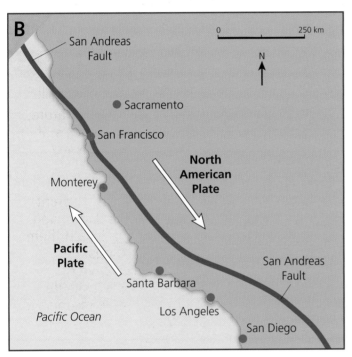

Meeting of North American and Pacific plates

power of the plates there is continual jarring, which sets off the daily earth tremors recorded in the region (see map **A**).

Occasionally the plates catch against one another for longer periods, as they release they set off massive earth tremors or **earthquakes**, such as those effecting San Francisco (17/10/89) and Los Angeles (17/1/94). The former measured 7.1 on the **Richter Scale**, the latter 6.6. This is known as the **magnitude** of the earthquake. Generally, the bigger the magnitude, the greater the damage.

STEP 1

1 What evidence is there on map **A** to tell us that California is an extremely active area of the world?

2 Write a short summary of the pattern of earthquake activity for the hour, day, and week shown.

3 Research on the Internet to check out present activity in the area (see Longman web site).

4 Describe what the San Andreas Fault looks like in real life using photo **C** to help you.

Homework

Use your school or local library to research the Richter scale. What effect would earthquakes of magnitudes 1, 3, 5 and 7 have if they were to strike your home region?

• research skills • summarising • descriptive writing •

Waiting for the Big One

Carl Nolte, San Francisco Chronicle reporter said, 'People often ask, "How can I tell when there is an earthquake?" Californians always answer, "You will just know, you will know."'

The earthquake of 1989 killed over 60 people, injured more than 2,500 and left over 10,000 homeless. It is estimated that the clean up cost was over $8billion. It was the biggest earthquake in this particular area since the famous earthquake of 1906, which measured 8.3 and had a catastrophic impact. Just look at Jack London's record (source **B**).

Research on the pattern of plate movement and fault activity by scientists in the area indicates that there is a 75% chance of a massive earthquake striking the region before 2030.

Jack London's initial comments on the impact of the earthquake, April 1906

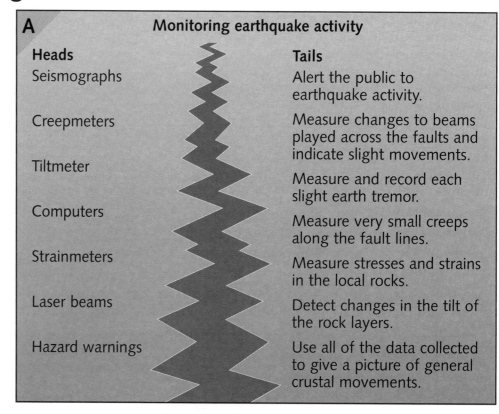

A   Monitoring earthquake activity

Heads	Tails
Seismographs	Alert the public to earthquake activity.
Creepmeters	Measure changes to beams played across the faults and indicate slight movements.
Tiltmeter	Measure and record each slight earth tremor.
Computers	Measure very small creeps along the fault lines.
Strainmeters	Measure stresses and strains in the local rocks.
Laser beams	Detect changes in the tilt of the rock layers.
Hazard warnings	Use all of the data collected to give a picture of general crustal movements.

B

San Francisco is gone. Nothing remains but memories and a fringe of dwelling – houses on its outskirts. Its industrial section is wiped out. Its business section is wiped out. The factories and warehouses, the great stores and newspaper buildings, the hotels and palaces are all gone. Within an hour after the earthquake, the smoke of San Francisco's burning was a lurid tower visible a hundred miles away.

STEP 2

1 Look at table **A** and match the heads to the tails. Use the information to help you to describe some of the ways scientists keep track of earth movements in areas like California.
2 Earthquakes can strike at any time of the day, there is no set pattern. People in California are advised to have an earthquake survival pack ready which they can take with them in case of an emergency. Write a list of the items that you would include in your survival pack and say why you have included them.

Extension

If Jack London were alive at the time of the next big earthquake in San Francisco Bay area, how might he report the event? For example: 'April 16th 2024, I look across San Francisco Bay after the "Big One". . .'

Spot the pattern

The Earth's **crust** is not a complete layer. It is made up of pieces (plates) which fit together rather like the pieces of a jigsaw puzzle. Where the pieces meet are our plate boundaries, for example, down the west coast of America and in the mid Atlantic Ocean.

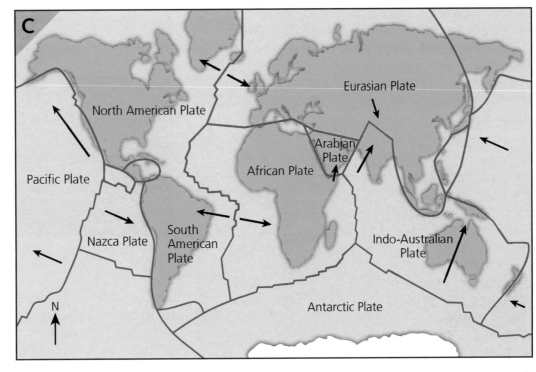

Plates, plate boundaries and direction of movement

STEP 3

1 Look at map **C** carefully. Name the major plates.
2 Which plate does the UK stand on?
3 List five pieces of information about the pattern of the plate boundaries. The first is done for you: 'One boundary runs all the way down the western side of North and South America.'
4 Look at the list opposite of ten earthquakes and volcanoes. Use an atlas to help you mark them carefully onto a copy of a map showing the plate boundaries. What do you notice about the pattern of earthquakes and volcanoes that you have recorded? Give reasons for your answers.

Earthquakes	Volcanoes
N. India Jan. 2001	Popocatepetl (Mexico) Jan. 2001
El Salvador Jan. 2001	Mayan (Philippines) Jan. 2001
Turkey Aug. 1999	Montserrat Sept 2000
Afghanistan May 1998	Etna Aug. 2000
Iran May 1997	Krakatau May 2000
Japan (Kobe) Jan. 1995	Kilauea (Hawaii). Feb. 2000
Los Angeles Jan. 1994	Stromboli (Italy) Sept. 1998
Colombia June 1994	St Helens (USA) July 1998
Mexico City Sept. 1985	Hakkoda (Japan) July 1997
Italy Nov. 1980	Amukta (Alaska) Sept.1996

Extension

Use the Internet to find the location of more recent earthquakes and volcanic eruptions. Record these on your map as well. Do they fit the pattern that you have already discovered?

• description and explanation of geographical patterns • Internet research •

Getting to grips with plate boundaries

In California the two plates slide past each other along fault lines (see page 51). This is known as a **conservative** plate boundary. However, there are other types of boundaries, some where plates meet, others where they move apart. But why do plates move? Look at diagram **A**.

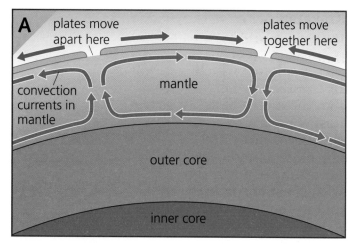

Diagram showing convection currents

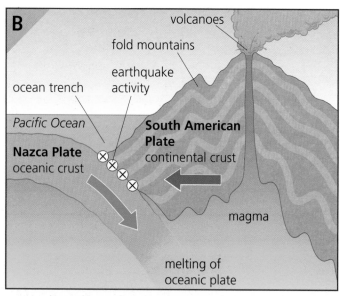

A destructive plate boundary, e.g.
S. America (west coast)

The crustal plates actually float on the **molten** rock of the **mantle** of the Earth. This is rather like an ice cube, or layer of oil floating on water. Molten rock in the mantle is heated up by the Earth's core. As it heats, it begins to rise towards the surface of the mantle (as peas rise to the surface in a pan of boiling water). As it nears the surface it cools and then begins to drop back towards the outer core, where it heats up and rises again. The molten rock moves in a circular pattern via a process called **convection**. It is the **convection currents** that cause the problem!

Where the currents move together we find **destructive plate boundaries**, and where they move apart we find **constructive plate boundaries**.

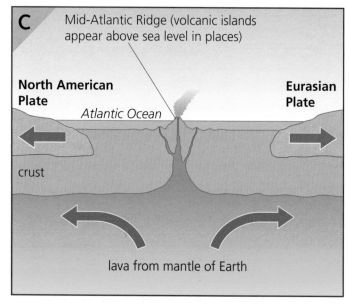

A constructive plate boundary, e.g. Mid Atlantic

Step 4

Using diagrams **B** and **C** describe what activity is taking place at each of the boundaries.

Homework

What are the main similarities and differences between these two types of boundaries? How are they both similar and different to the boundary in California?

  • interpreting diagrams •

Feel the force

Krakatau blows its top

If you look at diagrams **B** and **C** you will notice that volcanoes occur along plate boundaries. As with earthquakes, volcanic activity is constantly happening in certain areas of the world (active volcanic areas). Sometimes this volcanic activity can be devastating. For example, Krakatau in Indonesia (see map **D**) would not have been the place for having a tropical island holiday in the summer of 1883, when one of the biggest volcanic **eruptions** ever occurred.

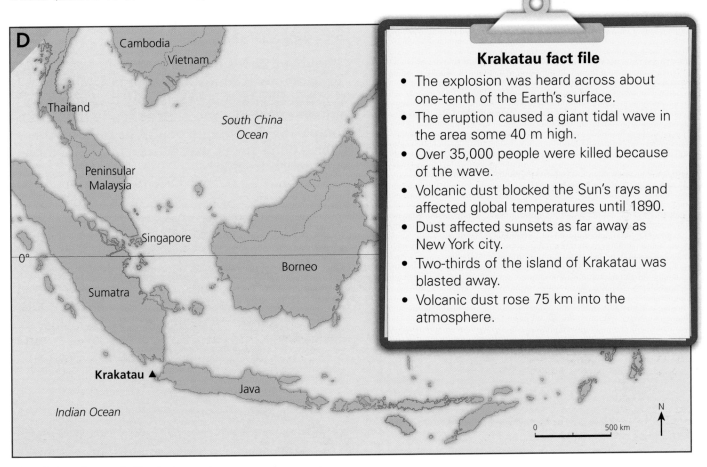

Krakatau fact file

- The explosion was heard across about one-tenth of the Earth's surface.
- The eruption caused a giant tidal wave in the area some 40 m high.
- Over 35,000 people were killed because of the wave.
- Volcanic dust blocked the Sun's rays and affected global temperatures until 1890.
- Dust affected sunsets as far away as New York city.
- Two-thirds of the island of Krakatau was blasted away.
- Volcanic dust rose 75 km into the atmosphere.

The location of Krakatau

Note

The explosion was much bigger than that caused by nuclear bombs dropped on parts of Japan at the end of the Second World War.

Some volcanoes are always **active**, such as those on the island of Iceland. Others are **dormant** or sleeping, such as Popocatepetl in Mexico – but do not trust them as they can still break into sudden action. This volcano had its largest eruption for almost 500 years in December 2000 (page 58).

Some volcanoes are dead or **extinct.** And yes, we did have volcanoes once in this country! Edinburgh Castle is built on the top of an extinct one.

Volcanoes also occur in certain locations called **hot spots** in the world, for example in Hawaii, where the crust is so thin that hot lava is able to punch a hole through it and flow out.

Rivers of fire

Spot the difference

Volcanoes are extremely exciting features, unless you live under constant threat from them! Volcanic eruptions can be very different in nature, some very explosive, and some just a constant trickle of very runny lava. The differences in the eruptions depend on:

- where the volcano is on the Earth's surface
- the pressure that has built up underground
- the temperature of the molten lava
- the amount and type of gases in the crust.

Although there are many different types of eruptions and styles of volcanoes the two main categories are **composite** (**strato**) volcanoes and **shield** volcanoes.

Composite volcanoes are the most common in the world, for example, Mt. St Helens in the USA, Mt. Fuji in Japan, and Popocatepetl in Mexico. Composite volcanoes are made up of layers of lava and ash. They build up into the **cone** shape that we all associate with volcanoes. The lava tends to be very sticky and builds upwards rather than flowing over very long distances.

Shield volcanoes are the largest in the world, for example, Kilauea and Mauna Loa on Hawaii. The lava is very runny and spreads out over vast distances. (It is really like comparing dropping porridge or milk on the floor – don't try it, just believe me – the milk runs much further!)

A

shorter distance than shield volcano

Steep sided, tall cone, layers of lava and ash, big crater, width of cone much smaller than shield volcano.

crater
vent
lava layer
ash layer
magma chamber

Cross-section of a composite volcano

A composite volcano, e.g. Etna

  • aerial photo and diagram interpretation •

Cross-section of
a shield volcano

A shield volcano, e.g. Kilauea

Gentle sides, fast flowing lava covers large distances – cone less tall but much wider than composite volcanoes.

larger distance

cone   crater
vent
lava flow

magma chamber

STEP 5

1 Use diagrams and photos in sources **A** and **B** to create a table which shows similarities and differences between composite and shield volcanoes.

Extension

Use your library or information centre to build up a simple case study of a composite or shield volcano of your choice. Before you start, write down a list of **key questions** that you want to answer, for example:

- Where in the world is the volcano located?
- What type of plate boundary is it situated on?
- Is the volcano active, dormant or extinct?

THINKING THROUGH YOUR ENQUIRY

'Active Earth'

Create an information booklet for Key Stage 3 pupils entitled 'Active Earth'. The layout and design of the booklet is up to you. However, it should include short summaries of the following items:

- evidence (using, for example, California) to show that Earth is a very active place, and that some areas are more active than others (Steps 1 and 2)

- ways in which people monitor and prepare for earthquake activity (Step 2)
- links between plates and activeness (Step 3)
- information on the different types of plate boundaries (Step 4)
- different types of volcanic activity (Step 5).

3c Tectonic processes
• Ready to blow •

- Why was the eruption of Popocatepetl a shock to many people?

- What effect do volcanoes have on the environment when they erupt?

- How do vulcanologists use information from past and present eruptions?

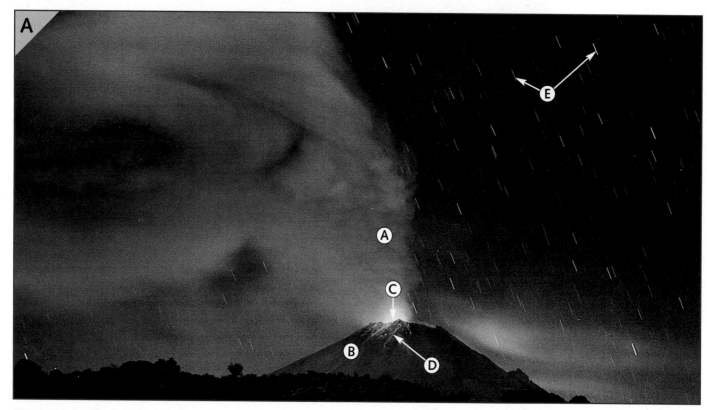

A

Popocatepetl spews smoke and ash into the night sky after it erupted for the first time since the Spanish arrived in Mexico 500 years ago

YOUR ENQUIRY

In this enquiry you will:

- investigate Popocatepetl, a composite volcano in Mexico which erupted in the late 1990s after a long period of inactivity, and the impact that it had on the local environment

- review the effects of eruptions in other areas of the world, using these to assess the risk to people living close to Popocatepetl

- investigate why it is important for people to study and be aware of different types of volcanic activity.

At the end of the enquiry you will prepare a short presentation for the local authorities on the character of a volcano like Popocatepetl, and the effects a big eruption or series of eruptions could have on people and the environment.

Getting to grips with the structure of composite volcanoes

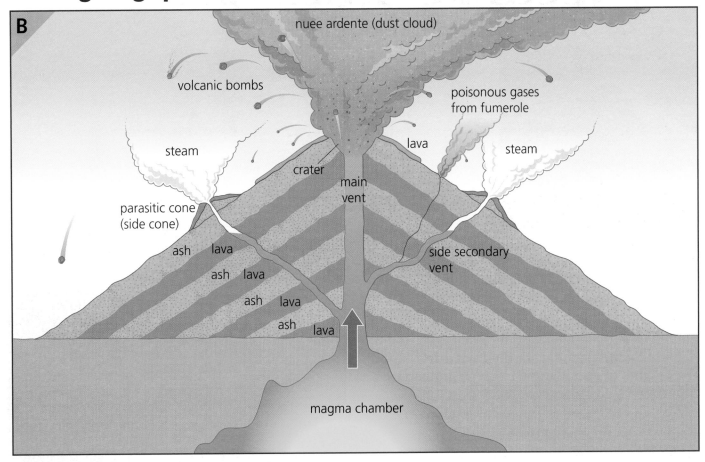

Cross-section through a composite volcano

STEP 1

1 Study photo **A** of Popocatepetl (Popo-Old Smokey). Match the following terms to the letters shown on the photograph:
cone shape   volcanic bombs   lava flow
crater   nuee ardente (dust cloud)
2 Draw a sketch of this composite volcano and mark these features onto it.

Homework

1 Imagine you were standing watching this eruption. Write down what you would say on a postcard home about it. Don't forget to think about sounds and smells, as well as what you can actually see. Geographical detectives use all these senses! You may wish to include a sketch on your postcard.

2 Study diagram **B** carefully. It shows a cross-section through a volcano. Use the information to write an A to Z of the composite volcanic features shown. Do not forget to explain what each feature is like. One is done for you.
Vent: Pipe taking molten rock (magma) from the magma chamber to the crater opening.

Extension

Use the Longman web site to research and describe a volcanic eruption that is presently taking place. Remember to think about key questions that you wish to answer.

Bubbling away

Aerial photograph of crater

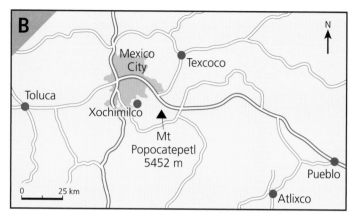

The location of Popocatepetl

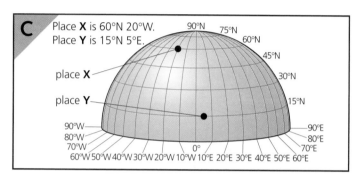

Locating places using latitude and longitude

The actual position of Popocatepetl is 19°N 98° 30'W. This is a little like a map reference. It gives the actual position of the feature on the Earth's surface (look at diagram **C**).

The first figure represents the **latitude** reading. The O° line of the latitude is the Equator. Popocatepetl is 19° North of the Equator.

The second figure represents the **longitude** reading. The O° line of the longitude passes through Greenwich in London so it is called the **Greenwich Meridian**. It is the line that time around the world is based on. Every degree is split into 60 minutes (shown by ' sign). 98° 30'W means 98° to the west of the Greenwich Meridian and half way to the 99° line.

Homework

Give the latitude and longitude reading of five of the volcanoes listed on page 53.

Give the latitude and longitude reading of five of the volcanoes listed on page 53.

D

Volcano forces villagers to flee

Residents at towns at the base of Mexico's Popocatepetl volcano were today evacuating the area after a massive lava shower that lit up the night sky like a firework show. The nearest villages, almost all now evacuated, are about four miles away. With sirens wailing, police drove through the deserted streets of Santiago Xalitzintla, one of the closest villages, shouting through loud hailers for the few remaining inhabitants to leave. Servando de la Cruz, a vulcanologist said, 'It could have been worse if this had been a brief, more extremely violent eruption.'

From *Southern Evening Echo*, 19th December, 2000

40,000 abandon their homes under the volcano

The Mexican army evacuated 40,000 people from their homes yesterday 19/12/2000 after Popocatepetl on the edge of Mexico City erupted twice. The 18,000 ft volcano threw rocks 18 inches in diameter up to 650 ft into the air, spewing debris across a 6 mile radius. A huge plume of incandescent lava was visible from 40 miles away. President Vincente Fox pleaded for calm, but added, 'We remain on maximum alert.'

From *Daily Telegraph*, 20th December, 2000

• using longitude and latitude to locate places •

Popocatepetl diary

Luis Martinez farms under the shadow of the volcano. The volcanic ash helps to provide very fertile soils, which means that the yields of maize are good. For years up until 1994 little evidence of volcanic activity was witnessed, but then the local environment changed dramatically.

E

Luis Martinez tends cornfields (maize) in front of Popocatepetl

STEP 2

1 Use map **B** to help you describe the location of Popocatepetl.
2 As the key vulcanologist in the area you are flown over the volcano (photo **A**). to help you with your work. What do you record? For example: steep sided, cone shaped . . .
3 Look at the diary of a local vulcanologist in source **F**. Create a table of activity impact for the period shown: in one column write down the volcanic activity noted, and in another the impact on people and the environment.

Extension

Luis Martinez farms in the local area because the soils are rich.

Through research in your library, list other advantages of living in volcanic regions, together with some of the disadvantages.

F

2000

January	Lots of ash coming out of the mouth. Moderate activity.
February	New volcanic dome forming in the old crater. Very active.
May	Smoke reaching 5 km in the sky. We have told people within 6 km to stay indoors. Choking conditions.
August	Some very explosive activity this month.
September	Early in month 30 minutes of massive activity one day, ash on many local settlements - even reached parts of Mexico City the capital. Some small earthquake activity as well. Late in month. Growing volcanic dome giving me great cause for concern. Will it be the big one?
November	Numerous eruptions this month including four on the 11th. Ash as high as 9.5 km. Landed on Santiago Xalitzinta down the road. Place in high risk zone 10 km around the volcano.
December	Hot volcanic bombs shot into the sky, pretty impressive firework display. Have moved 21,000 local people to shelters. 18th saw largest eruption for thousands of years. High zone now 24 km. We are worried about the glaciers melting and causing landslides.

2001

January	Earthquake activity this month, some measured 3 on the Richter Scale. Pyroclastic (super hot fragments) flows running down north side of volcano. One stopped only 8 km from Santiago Xalitzinta. Ash cloud immense.

Diary of local vulcanologist

Learning from past eruptions

The past is the key to the future. Vulcanologists study records of previous eruptions and their impact on people and the environment carefully to help to build up a picture of the likely impact of future volcanic activity.

A

AD 79 The cities of Pompeii and Herculaneum, which stood near Naples, were destroyed. Poisonous gases killed most people who were then, like the buildings, covered in hot ash and mud. Vesuvius was the volcano to blame.

B

May 1980 In Mount St Helens in the western USA a build up of gases and earth tremors trigger a massive explosion, which blows away a large part of the side of the volcano.

C

November 1985 Activity in Nevada del Ruiz, Colombia heats ice which then melts. This causes massive hot mud flows which sweep through the town of Armero killing over 20,000 residents.

D

1991 to 1993 Lava flows from vents of Mount Etna to the island of Sicily, creeping towards hillside villages and nearby towns. Troops try to divert lava flows away from them by building concrete barricades.

E

Mid 1990s Souffrier Hills volcano on the island of Montserrat in the West Indies gives out massive amounts of ash which covers large parts of the island. A large part of the island environment including Plymouth, the capital, is left uninhabitable and abandoned.

Keeping watch

F

Vulcanologists also keep constant watch over active volcanoes. Study of activity helps them to build up a clearer picture of what is and what could happen to people and the environment. They gather information, for example, on:

- changes in temperature around the volcanic region
- changes in pressure of gases found in, and coming from volcanoes
- increases in earthquake activity within an area
- changes in shapes of cones/domes
- emissions from fumeroles – if they stop, it sometimes means that pressure is building up elsewhere
- lava character.

STEP 3

1 What are the main differences between the eruptions shown in sources **A** to **E**?
2 As a vulcanologist working in the Popacatepetl area, how might this information be helpful to you?

Homework

Look at the information in source **F**. It tells us some of the items vulcanologists investigate. Write a series of sentences to explain why each piece of information is an important key to volcanic activity.

THINKING THROUGH YOUR ENQUIRY

'Volcanic activity'

People in the Popocatepetl district have become very worried about the recent activity. As the volcano has become more active many are experiencing events which they are not used to. As a leading vulcanologist you have been invited to Santiago Xalitzinta to give a presentation to residents about volcanic activity, and the impact that it can have on people and the environment.

Your presentation will be short and supported with overhead projector transparencies. You will need to include the following information:

- resumé of what has been happening in the area (Steps 1 and 2)
- information about the structure of a composite (strato) volcano like Popocatepetl (Steps 1 and 2)
- how vulcanologists monitor volcanoes and use information of previous eruptions to help to make predictions (what could happen within their area?) (Step 3).

4a Environmental matters

• Containers for Dibden Bay – a major decision •

- Where is Dibden Bay located?
- What plans have been put forward for developing this site?
- What different points of view do people have about plans for the bay?

Associated British Ports (ABP) have plans to build a large **container terminal** at Dibden Bay. This is an area of **reclaimed land** on Southampton Water, one of Britain's major estuaries. The plans have caused great discussion. Many people are worried about the impact on the surrounding area, parts of which are specially-protected zones.

A

1 Hythe waterside settlement
2 Hythe marina and housing development – on reclaimed land
3 Dibden Bay area for proposed new container terminal (280 ha)
4 Marchwood army base port
5 Marchwood village residential area
6 Existing container port
7 Western Docks (New Docks) developed 1920-30s
8 Deep water dredged channel to port
9 Eastern Docks (Old Docks) developed 1850-1920s
10 **Confluence** of the rivers Test and Itchen
11 Rural fringes of the New Forest (2000 seeking National Park status)
12 Southampton City region (220,000 people)

Oblique aerial view of Dibden Bay site on Southampton Water

YOUR ENQUIRY

In this enquiry you will review the plans and different points of view and then work as a team to create a report outlining whether you think that the new container terminal should or should not be given the go ahead. You will need to explain your decisions clearly.

Background to the issue

Southampton is a major port situated close to the English Channel, one of the world's busiest seaways. It is a major stop-off port, for example for boats moving between North America and mainland Europe.

Southampton is the country's leading cruise liner and car handling port. It is the second largest, deep-sea container terminal in Britain. The port handles over 35 million tonnes of cargo a year and is crucial to the UK's economy (e.g. handling half of all Far Eastern trade). It now handles more cargo than ever before.

The regional economy benefits by £1.3 billion annually, and 15,000 jobs directly or indirectly depend on the port.

The movement of cargo worldwide in containers is growing rapidly. New ships can be very large (see photos **B** and **C**), some being over 350 m long. Southampton is one of the few British ports that can handle these largest ships. The Southampton Container Terminal is very busy, but short of space, and with little room to expand to meet the expected massive growth in trade.

Along with others in the country, the port faces stiff opposition from European ports

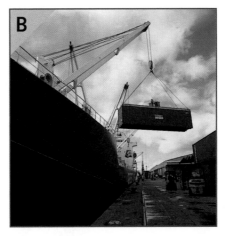

Southampton Container Terminal

NYK Procyon arriving at Southampton

such as Le Havre, Antwerp, Rotterdam and Hamburg. Shipping companies will use these ports if facilities in places like Southampton are not big enough, and then shuttle goods across to Britain in smaller ships.

ABP are therefore looking to build a large new container port with six berths on land it acquired in 1967 at Dibden Bay. This would not only allow the port to handle more large ships, but also create an expected 3,000 new jobs in the area.

Dibden Bay is an area of land reclaimed from the sea by in-filling with materials dredged from other parts of Southampton Water. It is considered by many to be a brownfield site, which is presently open space. Use of reclaimed land along the estuary for building docks is not new. The old and new docks and existing container terminal are all built on it (see photo **A**).

STEP 1

1 Use your atlas to describe the location of the port of Southampton.
2 Using photo **A** to help you, describe the location and character of Dibden Bay.
3 In groups, look at all the photo sources and information. Discuss why a new container terminal might be needed. Write five sentences to summarise your reasons.

Extension

Research in your library why Southampton has grown as a major port. Draw an annotated sketch map to show your results.

Dibden Bay container terminal proposals

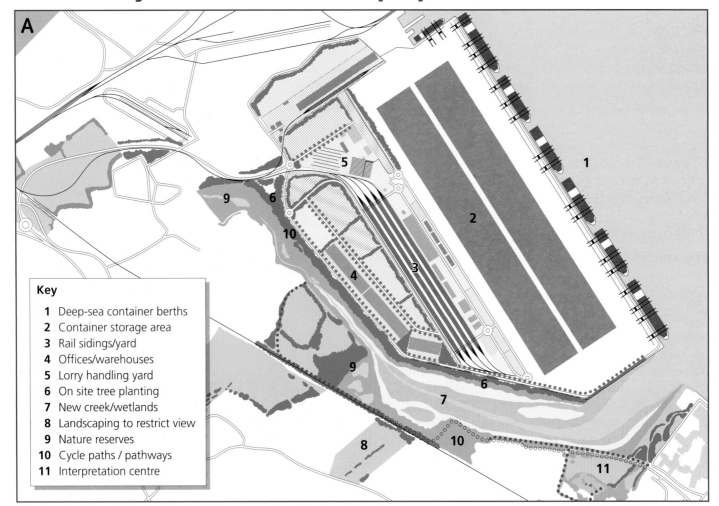

A

Key

1 Deep-sea container berths
2 Container storage area
3 Rail sidings/yard
4 Offices/warehouses
5 Lorry handling yard
6 On site tree planting
7 New creek/wetlands
8 Landscaping to restrict view
9 Nature reserves
10 Cycle paths / pathways
11 Interpretation centre

Container terminal layout proposals

Some considerations

- Increase in traffic on roads and railways
+ Port has experience and expertise in handling container traffic
+ Much of the **infrastructure** needed is already in place
- Much of the area (mudflats and grassland) is environmentally sensitive
+ If ships drop containers overseas, goods would have to be imported from foreign ports increasing costs
+ Close to major shipping lanes 28 nautical miles away
- Lengthy construction time would affect the lives of local people
+ New port would create lots of jobs, but no new port might mean loss of jobs
- Pollution concerns, such as noise, visual and water
+ ABP owns the site already and it has invested time and money on it
- Close to the edge of the New Forest, an area of outstanding natural beauty.

STEP 2

1 The site information opposite is in rather a jumble. Unravel the jumble to create a list of advantages and disadvantages of the Dibden Site.
2 Use map **A** to help you to describe the layout of the proposed new terminal.

Dibden environment

New container terminal from Hythe Marina

New container terminal from Southampton Water

Proposed 'artificial' creek between Hythe and Dibden Bay

Mudflats like those exposed at low tide along Southampton Water are considered to be among the richest and most diverse ecosystems in the world. They are important feeding grounds for resident and visiting birds. Due to this they are listed as Special Protection Areas (SPAs).

The area of reclaimed land is also important as an open space and wildlife retreat. It is given the status of Site of Importance for Nature Conservation.

A major dilemma

EU rules say that these sites should only be developed if it is crucial to the needs of the country. Supporters of Dibden Bay argue that the new port is vital to the economy of the region and country.

If ABP are given the green light to build the port, extensive landscaping of the surrounding area will take place (see map **A**). This would be done in partnership with environmental and wildlife organisations, and include a new tidal inlet and mud flat area. New glades and hedgerows, a nature reserve, picnic sites, shoreline trails, view points, footpaths and cycleways are also planned.

STEP 3

1 Look at the artist's impressions of the completed terminal. What are your opinions about the impact it could have on the local environment? Are your views similar to those of other people in the class?
2 Using the information on this spread, list some of the steps people might take to protect the environment if the port were built. What steps might you include?
3 Why is Dibden such an environmentally-sensitive location?

Homework

Tell people in your family what you know about the proposals for Dibden Bay. What are their opinions about the scheme?

Opinions are so divided

A

I have worked in the docks for 30 years, my grandfather did before me, and my sons are over in the Old Docks at the moment. We really do need the new terminal otherwise I think the port will slowly die.

Port Worker

This is a very big decision as the port now stands at a crossroads. If we cannot expand to meet demand, ships will take their trade to ports outside of the UK, which have their own well-advanced expansion plans.

Port Executive

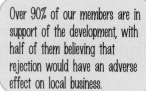

The planned expansion at Southampton is of strategic importance to the UK and the region. It must be supported through its planning stages.

CBI

ABP have to prove that there is a clear need for this new port, and that there are not locations that are more beneficial to the UK such as Shellhaven and Felixstowe in Essex.

Member Residents against Dibden Bay Port

Over 90% of our members are in support of the development, with half of them believing that rejection would have an adverse effect on local business.

Southampton Chamber of Commerce Member

The planned development is a must. Southampton is the country's 'Gateway to the World', this position must be protected.

Southampton City Councillor

We are especially concerned about the impact on the New Forest, especially when you consider it is set to become the first National Park in the south-east.

Council for National Parks

I think that new dredging and development will kill off the oyster industry along the water.

Local Oyster Fisherman

If it is built, life in and around our village will never be the same. I think that it would have a disastrous impact on the place and people who live here. They would have to up grade the roads and railway lines around here to cater for all of the extra traffic the port would create.

Marchwood Resident

What is the point of having nature conservation if developments that would harm a site, given top European Protection, go ahead?

Friends of the Earth Rep.

STEP 4

Read the comments made about the proposed new port by people who live in area. List the people who are for the scheme and those that are against it. Write down what you consider to be the most important reason for: **a)** wanting the port developed, **b)** opposing it.

Homework

Suggest what views the following people might have about the scheme: a local bird watcher, resident of Hythe marina complex, local lorry company manager, local building contractor, local yacht club owner, a local electronics importer.

Decision time

In this country there are strict planning procedures which must be followed in the case of proposed developments such as Dibden Bay. This includes a **public inquiry** which allows groups, from both for and against the scheme, to express their point of view fully (e.g. Residents Against Dibden Bay Action Group). At the end of the inquiry the chairperson will consider all the points of view and put their findings to the Secretary of State for the Environment (representing the Government) for the final decision.

Although the time scale opposite has been suggested, it is clear that the inquiry might take much longer than expected because of the number of cases to be put forward.

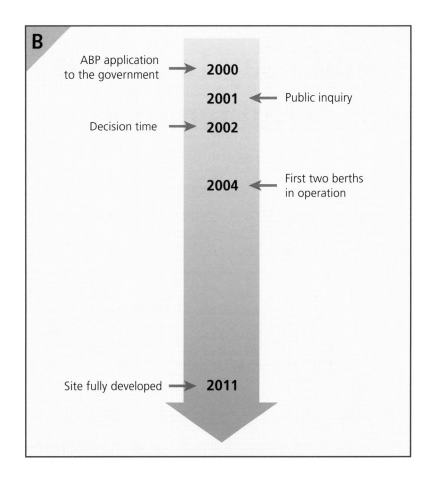

B

ABP application to the government → **2000**

2001 ← Public inquiry

Decision time → **2002**

2004 ← First two berths in operation

Site fully developed → **2011**

Suggested time scale

THINKING THROUGH YOUR ENQUIRY

'Should the port go ahead?'

The chair of the inquiry has a big weight on his shoulders. He must come to the correct decision as to whether the port should or should not get the go-ahead. Can you help him?

Work in groups to prepare a short report that outlines the proposals. You may wish to include maps and diagrams in your report to help to back up the points you make. The content and style of your group report is up to you to decide upon, but may well include:

- information about the location of the Dibden Bay site (Step 1)

- why ABP wish to build on the site (Step 1)
- a summary of what the port authorities wish to build (Step 2)
- information about the environmental impact of development (Step 3)
- a summary of views for and against the scheme (Step 4)

It would be very helpful if you were to write a conclusion saying whether your group feels that the green light for development should, or should not be given. Do not forget to give detailed reasons for your decision.

• And I say to myself – what a wonderful world •

- What opinions do you have about landscapes?

- Why was Yosemite given National Park status?

- What is Yosemite National Park like in character?

- What demands do tourists place on areas like Yosemite?

A

Oh, yes I went to the white man's school.
I learned to read from schoolbooks, newspapers and the Bible.
But in time I found that these were not enough.

Civilised people depend too much on man-made printed pages.
I turned to the Great Spirit's book which is the whole of creation.
You can read a big part of that book if you study nature.

You know, if you take all your books, lay them out under the sun, and let the snow and rain and insects work on them for a while, there will be nothing left.

But the Great Spirit has provided you and me with an opportunity for study in nature's university, the forests, the rivers, the mountains and animals which include us.

Tatanga Mani, Stoney Nation Chief

YOUR ENQUIRY

In this enquiry you will:

- discover your own feelings and those of others towards landscapes
- investigate the character of Yosemite, a wilderness area in California USA
- discover how Yosemite is managed to ensure that the quality of the environment is sustained
- look at some of the recreational demands that are placed on it.

In the final enquiry you will be asked to construct a spread of two A4 pages on Yosemite National Park. Your work is to be placed by a travel firm in their new tourist brochure advertising holidays in the USA. It will be included in a coach tour holiday entitled 'Wonderful western wildernesses'.

Magical landscapes stateside

View of the Golden Gate Bridge San Francisco

Death Valley California

Near Monument Valley Utah

Trans-America Pyramid
San Francisco

Grand Canyon Arizona
from the south rim

Mammoth Lakes California

STEP 1

1 Tatanga Mani was a **Native American** who had strong views about the environment (source **A**). Work with a group of your friends to try to unravel his feelings. Share your group's thoughts with the class.

2 Look at photos **B** to **G** above. Describe each of the landscapes. List them in order from your most to least favourite. Give reasons for your choices. How do they compare to the feelings of other people in your class? Is there a pattern to the lists?

Homework

Why do you think that is important to protect landscapes such as those shown in the photographs above?

Extension

Using maps, sketches, diagrams and written information, create an A3 poster of places that you like and dislike within the area that you live.

Off to Yosemite

Simple base map of Yosemite National Park

'Yosemite evokes a sense of inspiration, wonder and mystique. Some call it magical. Among the Earth's distinctive places, this showcase occupies a special part in the human spirit.'

Leonard McKenzie, Park Naturalist

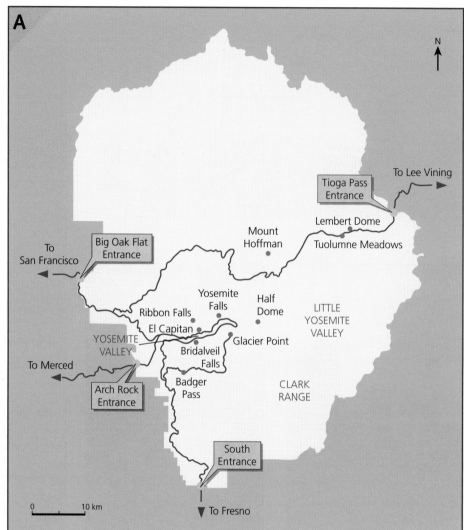

The location of the National Parks of California

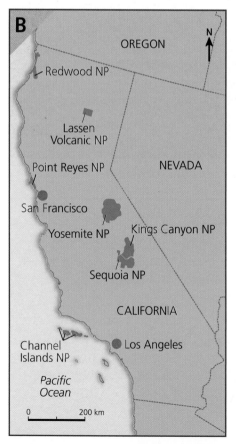

Yosemite is situated in the Sierra Nevada mountains in the state of California (see map **A** and **B**). It is one of 350 or more areas given **National Park** status across the USA. The process of naming it as one of the parks took place in Congress on 1st October 1890. The first park to be designated was Yellowstone (of that **geyser** Old Faithful fame) in the state of Wyoming. Areas were given National Park status to help to protect their outstanding natural beauty for future generations. Some of the parks are so important and unique that they have been granted **World Heritage Site** status by the United Nations.

The pattern of conserving open spaces through granting of National Park status has happened in the UK as well, with the Peak District, Lake District, Dartmoor and Snowdonia becoming parks in 1951.

Yosemite covers an area of 302,694 **hectares** (Lake District UK largest is 229,198 hectares).

• map and photo interpretation • citizenship • Internet research •

Yosemite portrait gallery

Half Dome from Glacier Point

Tuolumne Meadows

El Capitan Rocks

'Yosemite is the grandest of all the special temples of Nature. As long as I live, I will ever after hear waterfalls, and birds and winds sing. I'll acquaint myself with the glaciers, and get as near to the heart of the world as I can.'

John Muir, a Scotsman who settled in Yosemite

Yosemite Falls

Floor of the Yosemite Valley

STEP 2

1 Describe the location of Yosemite National Park using map **B** and an atlas.
2 Photos **C** to **G** have been selected to be included in a new tourist guidebook on Yosemite. Write down the caption you would include by each photograph. (Your captions should capture the magnificence of the area. The words of Muir and McKenzie might help you.)

3 Why do you think Yosemite was made a National Park in 1890?

Extension

Some places have been designated as World Heritage Sites. Research for and name two in the USA. Why are these places so extra special?

The shaping of Yosemite

Yosemite is best known for its fantastic valleys, magnificent **granite** domes, waterfalls, giant **sequoias** and spectacular mountain wilderness, but what processes shaped this landscape?

A

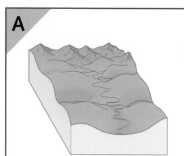 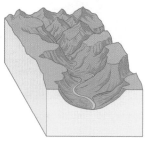 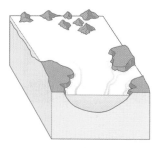 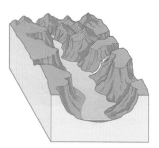

A **50 million years ago** The River Merced running through gently rolling hills with tributary streams joining it.

B **10 to 3 million years ago** Earth movements force up the land to create the Sierra Nevada mountains. The Merced River cuts out a deep canyon-like. valley.

C **1 million to 25,000 years ago** Glaciers fill the main valley and side ones, deepening and widening them. Some glaciers are up to 2,150m deep.

D Melting glaciers leave behind a very deep valley and glacial lakes. Waterfalls cascade down from hanging valleys. The floor of these tributary valleys now hang high above the main valley, because the glaciers in them were not as powerful, and erosion not so great. Glaciers left their mark in other ways such as by carving roche moutonnées (see photo B).

B

Lembert Dome

The formation of Yosemite landscapes

STEP 3

1 Use the sources on this page to describe and explain the physical processes that have created the Yosemite landscape of today.
2 Yosemite is now a major recreational area. What human processes would you expect to be affecting the landscape (e.g. the trampling of plants by walkers)? Map **C** will give you some clues.

Extension

Look at the photograph of Lembert Dome carefully. The feature is a glacial feature called a **roche moutonnée**. Draw a labelled field sketch to show the main features of the dome. How do you think this may have been formed?

  • diagram interpretation • explanatory writing •

C

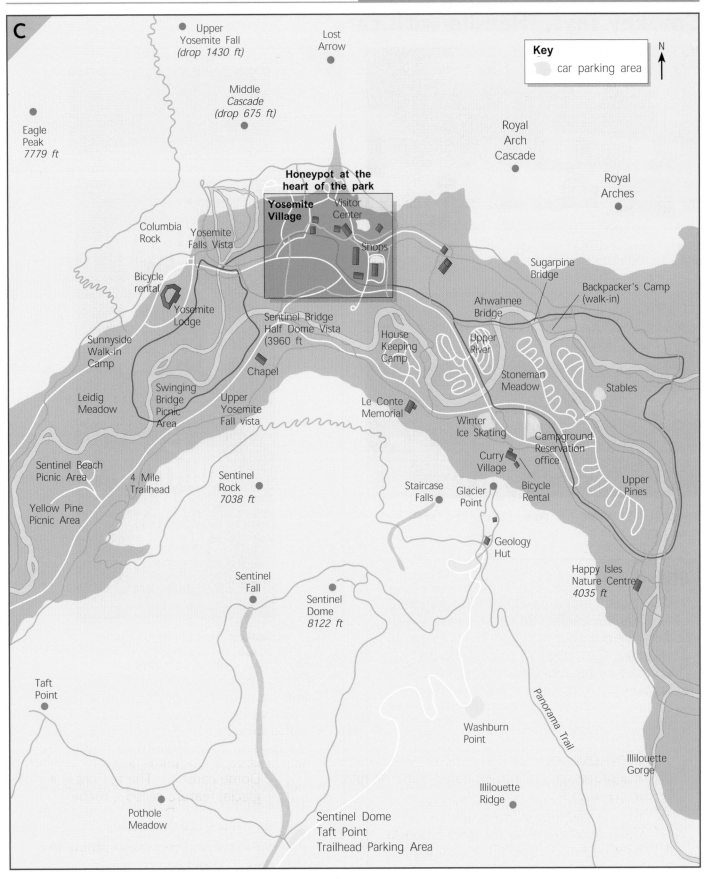

Upper
Yosemite Fall
(drop 1430 ft)

Lost
Arrow

Middle
Cascade
(drop 675 ft)

Royal
Arch
Cascade

Eagle
Peak
7779 ft

Royal
Arches

Key

car parking area

N

**Honeypot at the
heart of the park**

Columbia
Rock

**Yosemite
Village**

Visitor
Center

Yosemite Falls Vista

Shops

Sugarpine
Bridge

Backpacker's Camp
(walk-in)

Bicycle
rental

Ahwahnee
Bridge

Yosemite
Lodge

Sentinel Bridge
Half Dome Vista
(3960 ft

House
Keeping
Camp

Upper
River

Stoneman
Meadow

Stables

Sunnyside
Walk-in
Camp

Chapel

Upper
Yosemite
Fall vista

Le Conte
Memorial

Winter
Ice Skating

Leidig
Meadow

Swinging
Bridge
Picnic
Area

Curry
Village

Campground
Reservation
office

Upper
Pines

Sentinel Beach
Picnic Area

4 Mile
Trailhead

Sentinel
Rock
7038 ft

Staircase
Falls

Glacier
Point

Bicycle
Rental

Yellow Pine
Picnic Area

Geology
Hut

Happy Isles
Nature Centre
4035 ft

Sentinel
Fall

Sentinel
Dome
8122 ft

Taft
Point

Washburn
Point

Panorama Trail

Illilouette
Gorge

Pothole
Meadow

Illilouette
Ridge

Sentinel Dome
Taft Point
Trailhead Parking Area

Tourist facilities in Yosemite close to the park centre

Smokey says, 'Handle with care'

Vehicles entering the park through the Tioga Pass

Yosemite Village in summer (packed with tourists)

Step 4

1 Construct a graph to show visitor numbers to Yosemite since 1984 using source **C**. Describe the pattern shown by your graph.
2 Use map **C** on page 75 to describe the tourist facilities found in Yosemite Valley.
3 Smokey helps to enforce the rules for visitors. Why is it important to have simple visitor rules and regulations?

Homework

In the UK we have no 'Smokey', but we do have a simple countrycode that we are asked to follow when we are in open spaces. Use your school or local library to discover what is included in this code.

C	Visitor numbers	
1984		2.84 million
1990		3.23 million
1995		4.10 million
2000		3.75 million

Smokey Bear (The US Parks official watchdog)

Smokey encourages people visiting Yosemite and other parks to sustain the environment by:

- not damaging or removing any of the natural or historic features (take only pictures, leave only footprints)
- not feeding the animals (some like the Black Bear can bite back!)
- keeping to the marked trails
- placing litter and recyclable items in the correct 'trash cans'.

Spreading visitors out

Many major cities are within easy travelling distance of Yosemite (see source **E**). The total population of these cities runs into many millions. There would be a major problem if everyone was to converge on Yosemite.

To meet the recreational needs of the region, and to take the pressure off parks such as Yosemite, other categories of protected open spaces have been created. For example there are over 250 smaller state parks in California. Many are on the coast (such as Big Sur in photo **F**), even closer to the major cities. The pattern is the same in the United Kingdom with, for example, **country parks** taking the people away from our National Parks.

E

San Francisco	184
Sacramento	164
Los Angeles	509
Reno (Nevada)	312
Stockton	114
Fresno	98
(1 mile = 1.6 km)	

Travel distances (in miles used in USA) from major cities to Yosemite Village

Big Sur State Park, California

THINKING THROUGH YOUR ENQUIRY

'Wonderful western wilderness'

As an expert on Yosemite National Park, you have been asked by a travel company advertising holidays in the USA, to create a two-page spread for their new brochure. It will be included in a section highlighting coach tours. The tour title is 'Wonderful western wildernesses'. The spread must help to persuade travellers that this is the trip for them, and Yosemite is the place to visit. The layout is up to you, and you can include any maps, diagrams and facts that you feel are important. You should, however, include information on:

• some of the magical landscapes one can visit in Western USA. You might wish to include personal comments about these (see Step 1)
• the location and character of Yosemite (see Steps 2 and 3)
• tourist facilities found within the park (see Step 4) – remember especially those that coach visitors could get to on a stopover.

Extension

Plan and undertake your own personal investigation into one of the National Parks of England and Wales (such as Dartmoor or the Lake District). (See the Longman web site.)

 • persuasive writing/creation of brochure spread •

4c Environmental matters

• Black gold •

- In what fragile environments is oil searched for and obtained nowadays?

- How do humans overcome severe physical conditions to move oil to the markets?

- What problems can be caused when the movement of oil goes horribly wrong?

We live in a world that places great demands on the natural environment, especially with regard to searching for and collecting natural resources. Oil is a crucial commodity (remember the petrol strikes of 2000?). It is often called 'black gold'. The search for new sources of oil, along with that for other resources (see Book 2, Antarctica) is moving to more distant and fragile environments.

Bush to use power of cuts as an excuse for Alaska oil drilling

Daily Telegraph

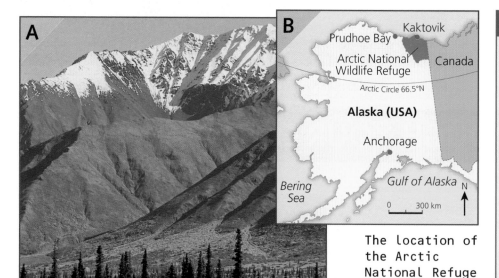

The location of the Arctic National Refuge

Tundra landscape in the Arctic National Refuge

YOUR ENQUIRY

In this enquiry you will:

- investigate some of the concerns regarding the search for, and the retrieval of oil from more remote and fragile environments
- look at some ways in which oil is moved from production area to the market place, and the problem of moving it by sea, especially when things go wrong.

At the end of the enquiry you will be asked to decide whether you are 'for' or 'against' the search for oil in, and movement across, fragile environments such as the Arctic. You need to prepare a list of your views in preparation for a class debate on the issue.

The search is on for new sources of oil

C

Californian power cuts push Bush

President Bush is using power cuts in California as a launch pad for expanding oil drilling in the country. The public are very angry about the cuts which have left the area in a 'state of emergency' for 16 days. They cannot understand why the richest state has had to spend £267 million of taxpayer's money to buy power from neighbouring states. They thought that the money would be spent on schools and transport rather than 'bailing out' electricity companies.

Mr Bush said that he was 'very concerned that demand was outstripping supply'. He said 'we've got to do something about it'. He was quick to talk about the need to drill more oil wells across the country and suggested starting in the Arctic National Refuge in Alaska. This comment 'attracted heavy criticism from environmentalists'. He has also been heavily criticised by his brother Jeb, the Governor of Florida, for plans for extensive searches in the Gulf of Mexico very close to the coastline of 'his' state.

Some people claim that President Bush and the oil companies are planning to vandalise the Alaskan wilderness. Others think that this is too simple a statement and that many of the indigenous population see oil as a lifeline.

D

Oil drilling equipment/tanks in a desert area

E

Oil-rig in very hostile seas – deep water

F

Oil drilling equipment in rainforest area

Step 1

1 Describe the location of the Arctic National Refuge (see source **B**).
2 Look at photo **A**. What is the **tundra** area shown like in character? (The extension activity below will give you the opportunity of discovering more about this ecosystem.)
3 Discuss in a group why some people are against the search for oil in the Alaska Refuge while others are for it. Share your findings with another group and note down the key points you discuss.
4 Look at sources **D** to **F** on this page. Why would the search for oil be difficult in these environments?

Extension

Use your library resource area to discover where the tundra areas of the world are, and what they are like in character.

 • tundra research • citizenship • sustainable development •

A hazardous journey

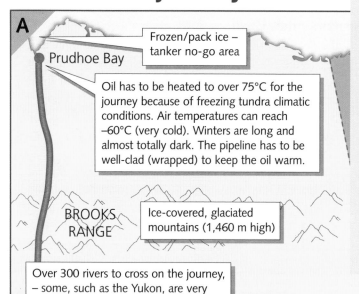

A

Prudhoe Bay

Frozen/pack ice –
tanker no-go area

Oil has to be heated to over 75°C for the
journey because of freezing tundra climatic
conditions. Air temperatures can reach
–60°C (very cold). Winters are long and
almost totally dark. The pipeline has to be
well-clad (wrapped) to keep the oil warm.

BROOKS
RANGE

Ice-covered, glaciated
mountains (1,460 m high)

Over 300 rivers to cross on the journey,
– some, such as the Yukon, are very
large. There are also many glacial lakes
to cross as well. Sometimes the pipeline
goes over the river, sometimes it travels
underground in a concrete casing.

Yukon River

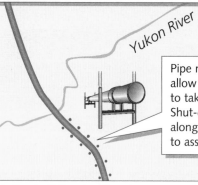

Pipe raised on stilts in some areas to
allow **caribou** to migrate. Planners have
to take care of the fragile habitats.
Shut-off, **fail-safe**, valves are placed
along the pipeline in case of leaks and
to assist emergency shut-down.

Active fault lines/earthquake zones to cross.
In 1964 an earthquake registering 8.4 on the
Richter scale hit Anchorage and Valdez with
a massive tidal wave. The pipeline has to
swing 6m horizontally, and 2m vertically to
cope with earth movements.

ALASKA RANGE

Bleak glaciated
mountains which rise
to a height of 6,000m.

Heavy snowfall, bleak
windy conditions, narrow
entrance from the sea via
Prince William Sound.

Anchorage   Valdez

The Trans–Alaskan oil pipeline route

In the mid 1960s vast amounts of crude oil
and natural gas were discovered in
northern Alaska, in the Prudhoe Bay area.
Because of thick **pack ice** in the Beaufort
Sea for long periods of the year it is
impossible for tankers such as the Exxon
Valdez to get to the oil fields to enable them
to move the oil to the consumers.
Consequently, an oil pipeline had to be
constructed to take the oil to Valdez (an ice
free port) on the south coast of Alaska for
shipment. Due to the environment of the
region, oil pipeline designers and builders
were tested to the limit (look at source **A**)
across the 1,300 km journey.

Alaska   North
America

Pacific
Ocean

Permafrost ground conditions: in winter
all the ground is totally frozen; in summer
the top layers only thaw and the ground
becomes very marshy, but below the
surface it remains permanently frozen.
This can cause serious damage to
pipelines and cause them to break.

B

Oil pipeline crossing Alaska

• diagram, photo, map interpretation • explanatory writing •

Bligh Reef traps Exxon Valdez

Valdez is situated on Prince William Sound. From the port a deep water channel takes tankers to the Gulf of Alaska and thence to the Pacific Ocean. It is a hazardous channel through the sound which is rich and varied in plant and animal life (sea otters, salmon, shellfish, whales and seals, etc.). The sound is also a key stopover for migrating birds. Hazards to shipping include floating ice, small islands and underwater **reefs** such as Bligh Reef.

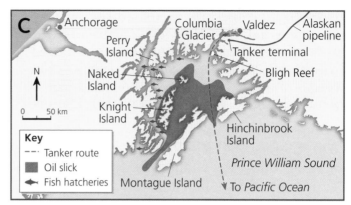

Prince William Sound – Exxon Valdez disaster

Prince William Sound area

E

'Ship aground on Bligh Reef – Losing oil – Need help.'

Radio message – just after midnight, Good Friday March 1989

Key points

- Exxon Valdez was a super tanker with 240 million litres of oil in 13 tanks.

- The tanker strikes Bligh Reef – oil leaks into the sea at 900 litres a second.

- The oil slick forms 10 cm thick, covering an area of 2,600 square kilometres (this is a massive environmental disaster).

- Slow organisation of clean up process – organisers fail to listen to the advice of the locals, especially the very knowledgeable local Indian peoples who work in the waters of Prince William Sound.

- The impact will be felt for years – over 300,000 sea birds (including loons, puffins and ducks perish).

STEP 2

1 Explain the problems facing companies moving oil from Prudhoe Bay in Northern Alaska to the port of Valdez.
2 Using map **C** and photo **D** describe the Prince William Sound environment. What effects will the oil spillage have on this area?
3 Work with a friend to make a list of the hidden effects of oil spills such as that in Prince William Sound. Divide your list into short-term and long-term effects.

Homework

What effect might the Exxon Valdez disaster have had on the following people in the region:

- eco-tourists
- oil workers in Prudhoe Bay
- local Indian lobster fishermen
- oil company directors
- fish hatchery owners
- ship pilots?

Extension

When oil tankers run aground and spew oil into the sea, clean-up operations swing into action, to clear oil from the sea and the local coastline if affected. Use your library/ information centre to research sufficient information to write an essay outlining some of the methods that have been developed to clean up affected environments.

Darwin's magical islands under threat

In 1835, Charles Darwin visited the Galapagos Islands. He was staggered to find an ecosystem that had **evolved** unhindered by humans, with many peculiar species that were found nowhere else in the world (see Book 2, Unit 3c, Borneo Adventure). The visit helped to inspire him to write about his theory of evolution, and in 1859 *The Origin of Species* was published. It did not go down at all well with many groups of people at the time, especially religious groups.

Galapagos pen picture

- The Galapogos islands are 1,000 km west of mainland Ecuador, in the Pacific Ocean.

- Ecuador makes much needed money from tourists, especially eco-tourists who visit Darwin's islands (over 100,000 per year).

- It is looked upon as an 'ecological Eden', one of the world's greatest environmental treasures.

- Animal life includes seals, iguanas, pelicans, boobies, sea lions, flightless cormorants, giant tortoise, rare sea urchins, sharks and whales.

The location of the Galapagos Islands

The *Jessica* on rocks off the Galapagos Islands

An iguana watches recovery work from rocks

'Go on then, evolve your way out of this'

E

Captain Arevalo takes the blame

Arevalo was captain of the *Jessica* carrying over 1 million litres of oil to the islands in January 2001. Captain Arevalo said that he misjudged the entrance into Shipwreck Bay outside the small harbour on San Cristobel Island. 'The truth is that I didn't even know that the rocks were there. It was over-confidence on my part. I am completely to blame.' Peter Vallejo the harbour master said, 'He will be judged once the investigation is over. He could face up to five years in prison.'

STEP 3

In mid-January 2001, the *Jessica* ran aground in the Galapagos Islands releasing its cargo of oil into the tropical waters and threatening a very remarkable ecosystem. Use all of the information given to you on this spread of pages to desk-top publish a short newspaper article on the accident and the possible impact of it.

THINKING THROUGH YOUR ENQUIRY

'Should we increase the search for oil in very fragile environments?'

Oil is a very precious resource (see Book 2 page 33). It is often called black gold. The petrol blockades across the UK in the year 2000 showed that many people were unhappy with the high price of fuel.

Oil companies are spending increasing amounts of money searching for new sources of oil in more distant environments, to ensure that they will be able to provide petrol and diesel to power the growing numbers of cars. You will probably want to drive in the future – perhaps there is an alternative? No cars!

Californians are getting angry at blackouts caused by an inability of power producers to provide power in some areas of the state. Because of this President Bush has put forward plans for companies to speed up their searches for oil in areas such as the Alaskan National Refuge. Some people don't like this – but they don't like having power cuts either. Perhaps there is an alternative!

The question: Does our class believe that we should or should not increase the search for oil in, and the collection from, very fragile environments of the world such as Alaska?

Decide where you stand (your point-of-view). Use all of the steps and information in this unit, together with your own personal research, to make a list of the key reasons for your stance. You might wish to pair up with one other person in your class who has a similar point of view.

Your points of view will be required when you take part in the class debate which will be based around the question posed above.

5a Brazil

• Slumming it in Rio de Janeiro •

- What are the poor's living conditions like?

- Why do these conditions exist?

- How and why do these conditions change over time?

Rio de Janeiro is Brazil's second largest city, with a population of over 5.5 million. It is located on the Atlantic coast and is surrounded by a range of mountains. This lack of room for expansion has restricted Rio de Janeiro's growth, causing overcrowding to occur within many parts the city. The rich live in luxury flats along the seafront where land prices are very high, while the poor are forced to live in those areas which are less desirable, e.g. on the steeper hillsides on the edge of the city, or wasteland near to industry. The areas of poor quality housing are called **shanty towns** – they usually start off as being temporary, but over time grow and become more permanent. There are huge contrasts between the living conditions of the rich and the poor. However, a lot of time and money have been spent in the poorest areas to try and improve some of the conditions.

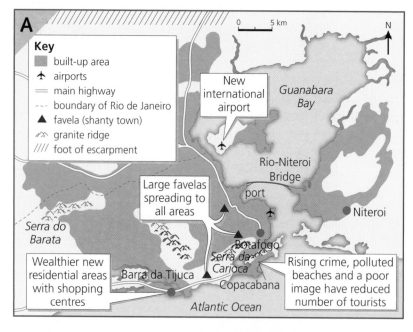

A

Key
- built-up area
- ✈ airports
- ═ main highway
- --- boundary of Rio de Janeiro
- ▲ favela (shanty town)
- ⌂ granite ridge
- //// foot of escarpment

0   5 km

N

New international airport

Guanabara Bay

Rio-Niteroi Bridge

port

Niteroi

Large favelas spreading to all areas

Serra do Barata

Botafogo

Serra da Carioca

Wealthier new residential areas with shopping centres

Barra da Tijuca

Copacabana

Rising crime, polluted beaches and a poor image have reduced number of tourists

Atlantic Ocean

Shanty settlement 40 years ago

Location of Rio de Janeiro

YOUR ENQUIRY

In this enquiry you will:
- describe and explain how and why the provision of services varies depending upon income levels and location
- describe and explain how this affects groups of people in different ways.

In your enquiry you will have to produce a TV documentary storyboard that identifies and explains the differences in living standards for people in Rio de Janeiro and explain what is being done to improve the lives of people there.

• drawing a sketch map •

Photos C and D show shanty settlements today

Photos E and F show rich housing in Rio today

STEP 1

1 Draw and label a sketch map to locate Rio de Janeiro.

2 Compare the types of housing shown in photos **C/D** and **E/F**. Include the following information about the houses: their size, shape, type and the materials built from. Describe what the surrounding area is like.

3 Look at photos **B**, **C** and **D** and describe how the shanty areas have changed over time. Think about the services they have, including: electricity, water, rubbish collection, sewage and shops.

Why do these conditions exist?

Rio de Janeiro has grown too quickly and as a result there are not enough resources available to help meet the increased demand for housing and basic services, such as water and electricity. Its population has risen quickly because of the high **birth rate** and number of people **migrating** into the city from the countryside, especially from the poor north-eastern region. This is called **rural** to **urban** migration. People are attracted to the richer industrial areas because they think they will get better-paid factory jobs and their **living standards** will be higher.

The rate of migration into Rio de Janeiro has begun to slow down over the past five years. This has given the government and organisations time to start improving the conditions.

STEP 2

1 Look at the data provided in table **A**. Give reasons why you think people moved from the NE to the SE.
2 The reasons why people leave or are forced from a place are called **push** factors. The reasons why people go to or are attracted to a place are called **pull** factors.
Look at diagram **B**. Draw a table to show the push and pull factors shown.

A	Monthly income ($)	Employed	Self-employed	Working in agriculture	Working in manufacturing	Working in services
SE	366	61.5%	19%	13.5%	24.3%	55%
NE	158	41.5%	27.7%	40.6%	13%	40%

B

Farming pays low wages and the hours are long.

Many people are evicted from their farm land.

Drought kills the crops.

There is better access to schools and hospitals in the city.

Poor soils produce low crop yields.

More opportunities in the city to make money.

Factory jobs in the city have higher wages.

Few services such as shops, schools and hospitals, no water or sewerage supply in poor farming areas.

Poor farming area contrasted with a rich city area

  • drawing a table • push/pull factors •

What is a favela?

Favela is the Brazilian word used to describe a shanty town. Usually the land is illegally squatted (people neither own it nor have permission to live there). They grow because the demand for cheap housing is greater than the supply of affordable homes. People are forced to build their own shelters from whatever they can afford or find. Today, over 1.5 million people live in over 600 favelas throughout Rio de Janeiro. Some may be very small consisting of a few houses, while others house up to 100,000 people. Houses are often crammed together leaving no room for footpaths or roads. Where street names or house numbers do not exist, post cannot be delivered or basic services such as water and electricity supplied.

Over time houses become permanent as buildings are improved and enlarged and basic amenities (e.g. water and electricity) are added. Many favelas are now over forty years old. Morro de Favela was started in 1897.

A

Rio has its problems, and they are enormous! A third of its population live in favelas. They are overcrowded and have very few basic services. There are few jobs and violence is commonplace. In many places drug gangs control the streets and lawlessness rules.

STEP 3

1 Look at the photos on page 85 and the information above. Write a paragraph to explain what it must be like to live in a shanty town.

From 1991 Census

Comparison between the city and favela dwellers

	City	Favela
Monthly salary ($)	701	205
Illiterate people	6.1%	15.36%
Inadequate sewage	8.9%	36.7%
Inadequate water supply	3.9%	15.4%
Average population density (km^2)	243	360
No rubbish collection	4.3%	21.2%

Homework

Make a one-roomed shanty house using a variety of materials found at home. The class could then build a shanty town. You could produce a sound track with the sounds you would expect to hear if you lived there. Look through old copies of the *National Geographic* or the CD-Rom and cut out photographs of shanty areas from around the world to add to your display.

Many of the people who live in these areas do not pay taxes and this means that the government does not have enough money to pay for improvements needed. Often schemes rely on help and funding from international governments, banks, charities or the local communities themselves.

STEP 4

1 Look at the different methods used to improve the quality of the lives of people living in favelas. List the different groups involved and explain why you think they got involved.

2 Why is the government not able to solve all the problems in the favelas without the help of others?

3 Describe how the housing in a favela will become more permanent over time.

B

Methods used to improve living conditions

Government organised, i.e. favela Neighbourhood Project 1974 	Street paving
	Removing houses in the path of mudslides
	Repairing and building small, new housing units
	Connecting sewerage, electricity and street lighting
Self-help and resident associations 	Helping friends and neighbours improve their homes, i.e. DIY scheme (adding extra rooms)
Organisations and charities, i.e. World Bank Cities without slums campaign 	Providing doctors and nurses
	Building schools
	Building and running orphanages

• empathy/literacy •

THINKING THROUGH YOUR ENQUIRY

'Living conditions of the poor in Rio de Janeiro'

You have been commissioned to make a 30 minute documentary for television showing the living conditions of the poor in Rio de Janeiro.

- You need to produce an A3 storyboard that outlines the sequence of shots plus a script.
- Each picture needs to have captions and be labelled to show the details you wish to get across to your audience.
- Remember to add timings to your storyboard.

Suggested structure for your storyboard:
- locate Rio de Janeiro
- show that it is a city of contrasts between the lives of the rich and poor
- identify where the poor live within Rio de Janeiro
- what conditions do they live under?
- how are the shanty areas being improved?

5b Brazil

• Brazil in a nutshell •

- What is the physical and human structure of Brazil?

- What regional differences exist within Brazil?

- How is development affecting Brazil?

Brazil's physical structure

Brazil covers an area of 8.5 million square kilometres. It is the largest country in South America and the fifth largest in the world. Brazil can be divided into four physical regions: the North-east, Amazon Basin, Brazilian Highlands and the Coastal Plain.

In order to study Brazil's **physical structure** we have to look at its climate, vegetation, relief, soils and raw materials.

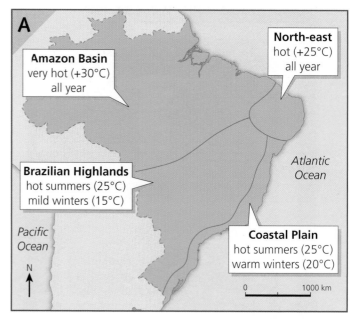

Physical regions and climate of Brazil

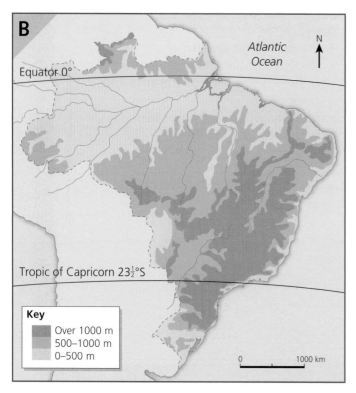

Relief map of Brazil

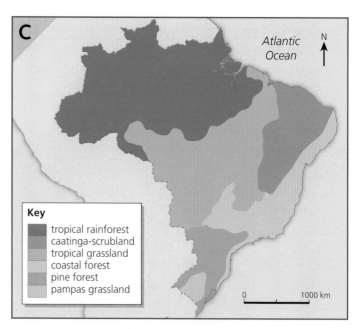

Vegetation map of Brazil

Throughout Brazil there are a number of different vegetation areas. Here both the type and amount of vegetation differs because the climate varies from area to area.

  • map interpretation •

STEP 1

1 Using an atlas, describe Brazil's location. Answer the
following questions:
  a What continent is it in?
  b Which hemisphere does it belong to?
  c What is its latitude and longitude?
  d What countries surround it?
2 Look at maps, **B** and **C** and an atlas. Copy and
complete the table below to identify the differences in
Brazil's physical structure between its regions.

	Relief/ natural features	Vegetation	Climate
Amazon Basin			
Brazilian Highlands			
North-east			
Coastal Plain			

YOUR ENQUIRY

In this enquiry you will:
- examine the regional differences that exist in Brazil
- describe and explain the physical and human features that give Brazil its distinctive character
- explain how Brazil is interdependent with other countries.

In your final enquiry you will use data to compare two regions of Brazil and explain how people's quality of life is affected by where they live.

 • completing a table • using an atlas •

Brazil's social structure

People from Brazil

Young people having fun

Watching time go by

Family from a rural area

Waiting for transport in the Amazon

In order to study the **social structure** of Brazil we have to look at its population totals, population **density** (the number of people per square kilometre) and **distribution** (where people live). We also need to look at the population structure (the age and percentage of males and females) and people's quality of life.

From IBGE Population Census 1991

E   Brazil's population structure

Years	Males (millions)	Females (millions)
0-9	18	18
10-19	17	17
20-19	14	14
30-39	11	12
40-49	8	8
50-59	5	5
60-69	3	2
70-79	1	2
+80	1	1

• population pyramid •

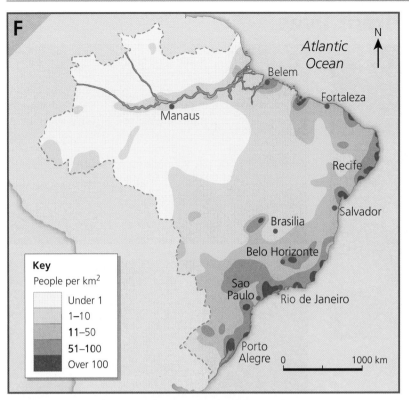

F

Atlantic Ocean

N

Belem

Fortaleza

Manaus

Recife

Salvador

Brasilia

Belo Horizonte

Sao Paulo

Rio de Janeiro

Porto Alegre

Key
People per km²

	Under 1
	1–10
	11–50
	51–100
	Over 100

0   1000 km

Population density map

The population of Brazil is 172 million and it is estimated that it will double within the next forty years. This is because the natural increase level is high (1.8), i.e. the birth rate is higher than the death rate.

In the past, people lived in rural areas and farmed for a living, e.g. in the North-east. However, over the past thirty years many have been forced to leave these areas because of the harsh physical conditions and **migrate** to towns and cities to find work or improve the quality of their lives.

Urban and rural populations in Brazil

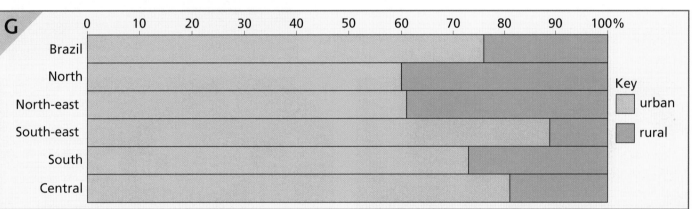

G

0 10 20 30 40 50 60 70 80 90 100%

Brazil

North

North-east

South-east

South

Central

Key
urban
rural

STEP 2

1 What is Brazil's total population?
2 Using the information in table **E**, draw a population pyramid to show Brazil's population structure.
3 Look at your population pyramid for Brazil.
   a Is it a youthful or ageing population (give reasons why you think this)?
   b Why is the population rising so rapidly?
4 Why are the physical conditions of the North-east described as harsh? Why does this force people to migrate from the area (think about the type of jobs they do)?

5 Look at map **F** and describe and explain the distribution of population in Brazil.

Homework

Select one region of Brazil and find out more about it. Go onto the Internet and research this area of Brazil. Imagine you are a tour guide in charge of a group of tourists visiting the area for three days. What would be your itinerary? Produce a leaflet for the English tourists which gives them all the information they need to know about the area.

Different people have different lives

People in a shanty town street and others selling fruit at the side of the road

Native people at work tending a small vegetable plot and sitting in their village

Person doing an office job and outside a luxury apartment

STEP 3

These photographs show how the quality of life differs for people living in Brazil.

1 Match the photographs to the following groups of people: unskilled migrants who are living in a shanty town, educated professionals living in a luxury flat in the middle of a city, an Amazon Indian family living in the Amazon Forest.

2 For each family describe their quality of life. You should think about: where and how they live, their type of house and what it is made from, the types of jobs they do, the services they use, the type of food they eat.

The economic structure of Brazil

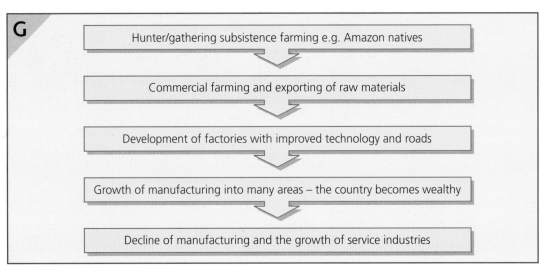

G

Hunter/gathering subsistence farming e.g. Amazon natives

↓

Commercial farming and exporting of raw materials

↓

Development of factories with improved technology and roads

↓

Growth of manufacturing into many areas – the country becomes wealthy

↓

Decline of manufacturing and the growth of service industries

The stages of economic development

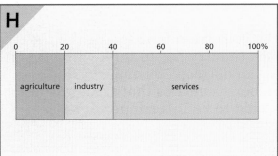

H

| 0 | 20 | 40 | 60 | 80 | 100% |

agriculture | industry | services

Brazil's GDP (by sector) 1999

In order to study Brazil's **economic structure** we have to look at the location and type of economic activity (primary, secondary, tertiary) that takes place. Brazil's economy has changed dramatically over the past 30 years. This has been described as an **economic miracle**. Brazil has the eighth largest economy in the world with a Gross Domestic Product (GDP – the amount of wealth created by industry) of $650 billion, making it the most important economy in South America. Brazil is often described as a **newly industrialised** country (NIC). Its economy is based on agricultural, mining, manufacturing and service industries. Many foreign companies have built factories especially in the South-east. They are attracted by the market size and the increasing demand for luxury items like cars.

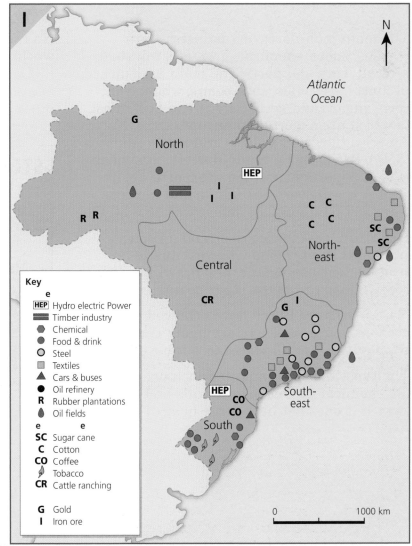

I

N

Atlantic Ocean

North

G

HEP

R R

Central

CR

North-east

C C
C
C C

SC

SC

G

South-east

HEP

CO
CO

South

Key

HEP	Hydro electric Power
	Timber industry
	Chemical
	Food & drink
	Steel
	Textiles
	Cars & buses
	Oil refinery
R	Rubber plantations
	Oil fields
SC	Sugar cane
C	Cotton
CO	Coffee
	Tobacco
CR	Cattle ranching
G	Gold
I	Iron ore

0   1000 km

The distribution of economic activities throughout Brazil

 • understanding economic development •

J	North	North-east	South-east
Area (%)	42	11	18
Average income (US$)	3,020	1,890	3,720
Industry jobs (%)	3	18	57
Farming jobs (%)	24	27	12
Population (%)	6.8	28	44
Population (under 18)	48	47	37
Density (per km^2)	3	27	67
Houses in urban areas with water supplies (%)	69	86	95
Electricity used in houses (kwh)	1,916	1,282	2,372

Regional disparities

The main manufacturing industries are textiles, shoes, chemicals, iron ore, tin, steel, aircraft, cars and parts. The main agriculture products are coffee, soya beans, wheat, rice, corn, sugar cane, cocoa, citrus and beef. Most of which are exported to Europe (28%), North America (23%) Asia (10%) and South America (35%). Brazil has a **trade deficit**, this means that it imports more than it exports, i.e. in 1998: exports were $51 billion and imports were $57.6 billion. The deficit was $6.6 billion.

Inflation, rapid price rises and a rising **national debt** (money it owes) due to its trade deficit has meant that Brazil has had to receive loans from the other countries.

Not all areas of Brazil have achieved such economic success. There are many **regional disparities** or differences (see table **J**).

The types of goods imported include: crude oil, chemical products, foodstuffs and coal (which it does not have large quantities of itself).

No country is isolated from the rest of the world. Each country has to work with others if it wishes to develop economically and become richer. Countries that trade with each other are said to be **interdependent**.

> ## STEP 3
> **1** Would you describe Brazil as a MEDC, LEDC or NIC? Give reasons to support your answer.
> **2** Use the following information to draw a pie chart to show Brazil's labour force by job type: services 42%, agriculture 31%, industry 27%.
> **3** Look at table **J**. Describe the differences which exist between the three areas. Which one is the most economically developed? Explain why you think this has happened.

THINKING THROUGH YOUR ENQUIRY

'Quality of life'

Look at the data provided in this unit. This will help you answer the following essay title:

'How and why does the quality of life for people living in Brazil vary?'
You may either compare two regions, or look at the differences that exist between rural and urban areas.

You may wish to use the writing frame below or produce your own.

Introduction

Brazil is a _____ _____ country. It has the _____ largest

economy in the world. Its wealth is created by a variety of industries including

_____. However, its level of industrial

development has not been the same in all of its regions. The _____ is more

industrialised than the _____. This means that regional disparities or

differences have been created. These include variations in job opportunities and wage

levels, which in turn affect people's _____ of life.

Words to help you: eighth, South-east, newly industrialised, North-east, quality

---

Paragraph 1 and 2

- Choose and locate an area
- Describe its physical, social and economic structure
- Explain why the area is more or less developed
- Explain how this affects people's lives
- Explain why not everyone has the same standard of living.

Conclusion

- Is it such a bad thing that differences exist?
- Can anything be done about these differences?
- If so, who should try to end the differences?

5c Brazil

• Can Brazil sustain its growth without harming its natural resources? •

• How is development affecting the natural environment?

• What is sustainable development?

• How can the environment be managed?

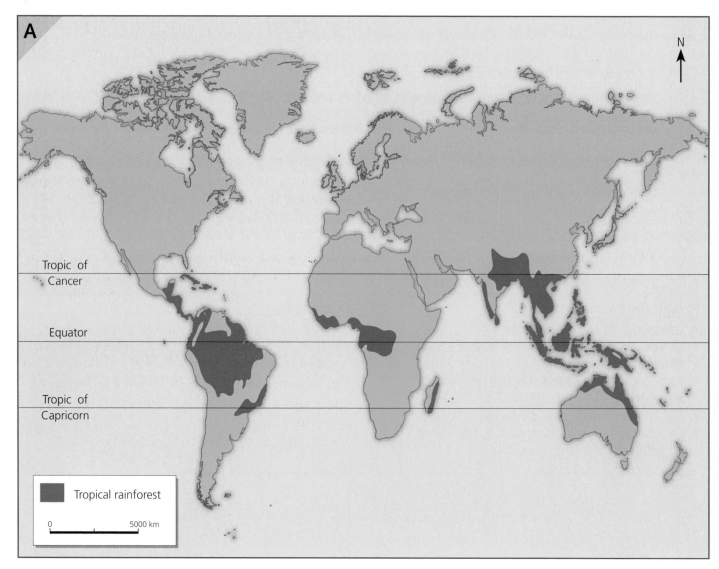

Location of rain forest

• map skills • understanding terms •

The Amazon rainforest's diverse environment

Tropical rainforests once covered 14% of the world's surface, now they cover only 6%. In less than fifty years we have destroyed over half the rain forest. The Amazon Rainforest is the largest in the world and accounts for 40% of what remains. It has been described as the 'world's greatest natural resource' – it is the home to 50% of the entire planet's animal, bird and plant species.

STEP 1

1 Describe the global distribution of rainforests.
2 What does deforestation mean?
3 Describe what had happened to the world's tropical rainforests over the last fifty years?
4 Look at photos **B** and **C**. Draw and label two diagrams to show how the forest changes once it has been deforested.

Homework

Find out what types of resources are found in the rainforest. Draw a poster to show why the rainforest can be described as the world's greatest natural resource.

An area of the rainforest that has been deforested

The Amazon Rainforest is home to many different types of plants and animals. It has over 55,000 types of plants, 428 species of mammals, 467 types of reptiles and 516 types of amphibians. It has the largest number of bird species in the world and still new species are being discovered.

Between 1972 and 1998 an area of the size of France (205,000 km) was cleared in the Amazon Rainforest alone. This is called **deforestation**, the removal of trees.

YOUR ENQUIRY

In this enquiry you will:

• describe and explain the causes and effects of deforestation
• recognise the different ways of managing the rainforests, including sustainable development.

In your final enquiry you will be asked to write a speech to explain what the global and local (Brazil) effects of deforestation are.

Why is deforestation occurring?

A

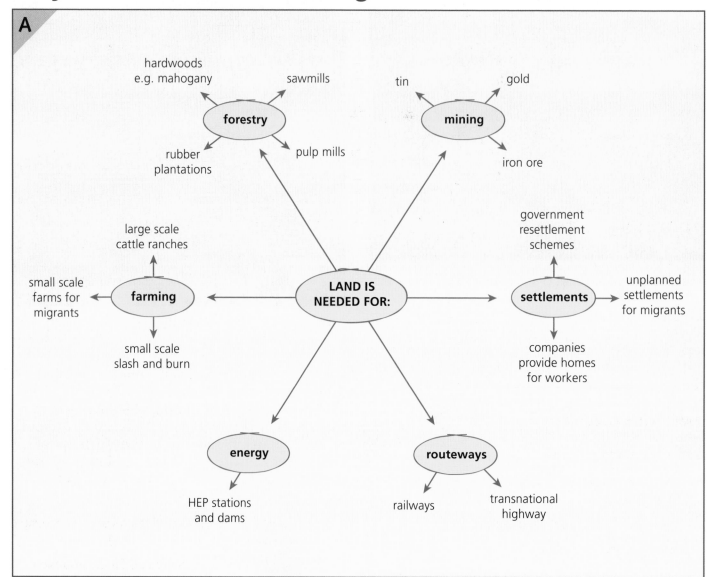

hardwoods
e.g. mahogany

sawmills

tin

gold

forestry

mining

rubber
plantations

pulp mills

iron ore

large scale
cattle ranches

government
resettlement
schemes

small scale
farms for
migrants

farming

**LAND IS
NEEDED FOR:**

settlements

unplanned
settlements
for migrants

small scale
slash and burn

companies
provide homes
for workers

energy

routeways

HEP stations
and dams

railways

transnational
highway

The causes of deforestation

The rainforest ecosystem is made up of many natural cycles including the water cycle, nutrient cycle and carbon cycle. These cycles are interconnected and work naturally together. However if one is affected then there will be serious knock-on effects elsewhere. Human activity is the greatest threat to the rainforests' existence in the future.

B

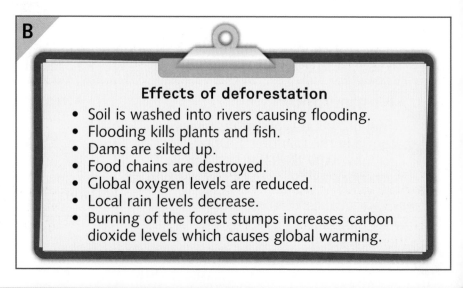

Effects of deforestation
- Soil is washed into rivers causing flooding.
- Flooding kills plants and fish.
- Dams are silted up.
- Food chains are destroyed.
- Global oxygen levels are reduced.
- Local rain levels decrease.
- Burning of the forest stumps increases carbon dioxide levels which causes global warming.

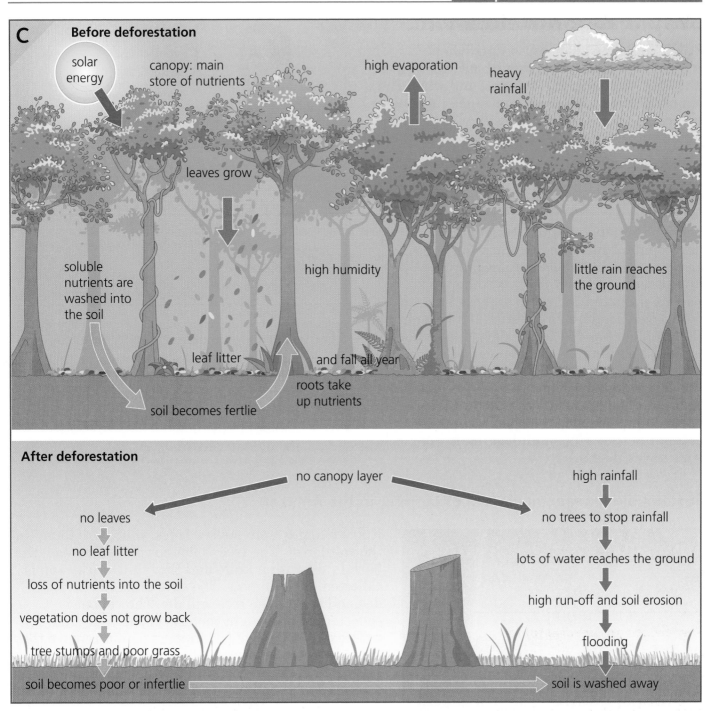

C

Before deforestation

solar energy

canopy: main store of nutrients

high evaporation

heavy rainfall

leaves grow

soluble nutrients are washed into the soil

high humidity

little rain reaches the ground

leaf litter

and fall all year

roots take up nutrients

soil becomes fertlie

After deforestation

no canopy layer

no leaves

no leaf litter

loss of nutrients into the soil

vegetation does not grow back

tree stumps and poor grass

soil becomes poor or infertlie

high rainfall

no trees to stop rainfall

lots of water reaches the ground

high run-off and soil erosion

flooding

soil is washed away

The breaking of the nutrient cycle

STEP 2

1 Look at diagram **A**. Write a paragraph to explain why the rainforest is being destroyed.

2 How is deforestation affecting the forest's nutrient cycle?

3 'Think Globally, Act Locally'. Produce a leaflet for the WWF to explain the effects of deforestation. Why should we care what is happening thousands of miles away?

Sustainable development

Sustainable development occurs when economic growth develops without wasting or harming the natural resources, and when the supply of these resources continues into the future. In this way, people in the future can maintain their present living standards.

People are able to earn five times more money collecting resources in a sustainable way, than cutting down large areas of the forest and not allowing it to **recover** or grow back to its natural state. Sustainable development has to be planned for and the environment has to be managed or **conserved**. In order for this to happen people, industry and governments have to work together. Growing national awareness of the problem has led to the development of the Amana Sustainable Development Reserve. This covers an area of 23,000 km². In 1998, the Brazilian parliament also introduced laws that were based on 'environmental crimes', in order to punish illegal loggers. It is estimated that 80% of all logging in the Amazon is illegal.

A

> We want to look at the forest as an opportunity for development, not as an obstacle to it.

Greenpeace campaigner

B

Activity taking place	The amount of money the land produces per acre ($)
Converted to ranching	60
Logging	400
Renewable and sustainable logging	2,400

C

Sustainable management methods
- Yields should be set and no more taken.
- Felling should be orderly and selected trees removed rather than whole scale removal.
- Enough trees should be left to allow the area to recover.

Sustainable management: rubber tapping in the Amazon

D

Rubber tappers

Rubber comes from rubber trees, which are found in the rainforest. The tree is not cut down. Instead, the bark is slit with a knife and the white sticky sap is collected in small pots. The slits must not be too deep otherwise the tree will die. The rubber is collected for only eight months of the year, from May to December. The rubber tappers do not remove the existing forest to grow rubber trees. Instead, they search for trees, which are growing naturally. The tappers do not collect sap from the same trees each day; they visit a tree every three days, giving it time to recover. There are now 63,000 families in the Amazon earning a living from rubber tapping reserves which the government has set up. To increase their income for the rest of the year they collect Brazil nuts and other fruits that grow in the forest.

• environmental issues • economic development •

E

The most detailed investigation of the fate of the world's tropical rainforest estimates that as little as 5% of the Amazon may remain in its pristine wild state by 2020. This is a result of an ambitious scheme, known as Avanca Brasil, to advance Brazil by building roads, railways and hydro-electric dams.

'To eat a pie efficiently you chop it into smaller pieces, which is what these developments are doing to the Amazon,' said an American scientist.

From *The Independent,* 19th January 2001 (adapted)

STEP 3

1 What does 'sustainable development' mean?
2 Why is sustainable development important?
3 What happens if the forest is not allowed to recover after it has been used?
4 Explain why rubber tapping in the Amazon is an example of sustainable management.
5 Give examples of the ways in which timber can be removed from the forest in a sustainable way.

THINKING THROUGH YOUR ENQUIRY

'We need to conserve the Amazon'

Look again at the photos on page 99 and the information on the causes and effects of deforestation.

You have to develop a web site. The aim of this site is to convince people there is a need to conserve the richness and diversity of the Amazon and explain why it needs to be developed in a sustainable way.

You may wish to use the following format:
- Identify the structure of the rainforest and explain what types of animal/plant live here.
- Outline the scale of global deforestation over the past fifty years.
- Explain why deforestation is happening.
- Identify the impacts that deforestation is having on both a local and global scale.

You may like to visit the web sites listed in this unit to get some ideas of the layout. If you cannot design the site on a computer, then take a plain A4 sheet of paper to show each screen and produce a wall display.

Extension

You may wish to use the Internet and other resources to see how other countries with tropical rainforests are being affected by deforestation and the schemes they are using to manage their forests.

6a Tomorrow's citizens

• Tomorrow's citizens – today •

- How do your actions affect the local area?
- Who makes the decisions about local developments?
- What is happening in your area?

What does it mean to be a good citizen?

We all have rights and responsibilities as citizens in our local area.

Dropping litter, making a noise, vandalism and damaging property can all make life worse for people in the local area. Clearing up an area, helping other people and contributing to local events can make life better. This enquiry looks at what individuals and groups can do to improve the local area.

Know your rights

YOUR ENQUIRY

In this enquiry you will:
- find out how local people can affect development in the local area
- describe how local government and national government can affect your locality
- explain what Agenda 21 is and how it affects local plans.

At the end of the enquiry you will find out what your local council is doing to address Agenda 21 issues and draw up your own vision for the local area.

Citizenship in action

What can you do to affect local planning?

If you think your local area needs a new development, like a skate park or community centre, how would you go about setting it up? You can encourage a local firm to build one privately or ask the local council. You might also be able to get money from the National Lottery fund. Many voluntary groups also raise money and help to improve the life of people and the environment in the local area.

What can you do if you object to a local plan?

In the UK we have the right to protest against things we disagree with. Some people are concerned over local developments in their area, like the building of new houses or the building of a new road. Some people take 'direct action' by sitting in trees and in front of bulldozers – and some of these are considered illegal. Thousands more join a campaign or protest group – these people go through a more complicated series of actions, but they are all legal!

In 2000, the government decided that 43,000 new houses were needed in south-east England – 13,250 of these were to be built in West Sussex. A plan to build 2,300 new homes near the village of Southwater was successfully challenged by the Southwater Action Group. Eventually the number was reduced to 550 new homes.

Protester against the Southwater development

C
How to organise a protest – action plan for rallying the troops

1 Keep your eyes open for new planning application notices in the local newspaper or stuck up near the planned development – they could be someone's new garage extension but it might be for a huge new housing estate!
2 Put the kettle on and call the neighbours – three or four committed people are needed to get things moving.
3 Make a plan of action.
4 Organise a public meeting to publicise the development and find out how many other people are interested in joining your group.
5 Write letters to local councillors, MPs and environmental groups – to try and get their support.
6 Contact the local press and organise a petition – you might also organise interesting events to attract publicity.
7 Organise events to raise money for letters, stamps and posters.
8 Get advice from experts, e.g. Council for the Preservation of Rural England (CPRE).
9 Be well prepared for meetings with the developers and planning enquiries.
10 Be prepared to negotiate or offer alternatives to the developers – it might mean you can change the plan to suit your objections.

From *The Times Weekend*, 17th June 2000 (adapted)

STEP 1

1 Suggest three things that an individual person can do to improve the local environment (see sources **A**, **B** and **C**).
2 Are there any recent local developments in your area that some people have objected to?
3 Are there any voluntary/community organisations working locally to improve your local area?
4 What have people done in your local area to improve the life of other people or the environment? How does your school support the local community?

What can the local community do to improve an area?

Your local community (whether it is a school, village, or 'local area' in a town or city) can also help protect and improve the environment, even if that 'environment' is mostly urban. Individual people can save energy and recycle things but **local councils** have to provide local **amenities** to help individual people and families do this (like the recycling bins in photo **A**).

Some councils are already providing different ways of collecting different types of rubbish to make it easier to sort and recycle.

A

Recycling bins

B

Meeting ends in chaos!

Last evening's town council meeting broke up in chaos when the leader of the council ordered police to clear the council chamber. Local people had spoken out strongly against the building of a new supermarket on the site of playing fields in the town. A local resident who lived near the site said that it would increase the noise from traffic and add to the litter problem. A local high street trader said it would mean the death of the high street, with shops closing and shopkeepers going out of business. Other people claimed that the town was already short of playing fields for the local young people and it would only add to the problems of vandalism and graffiti if young people had nowhere to go. After clearing the council chamber the local planning officer said 'It is a sad day for democracy when people can't debate an issue without resorting to shouting and abuse.'

Local **councillors** and **county councillors** vote on issues to do with town planning, transport, building and environmental issues. Everyone in local elections votes for these people. They are meant to represent the views of people in your local area. Do you know who these people are? Where do they meet and what do they discuss? In newspaper article **B** you can see what happened in one meeting.

Newspaper report on council meeting

C   **Local councils and counties can help protect the environment**

These are some of the ways they can make everyday life more sustainable:

- setting up cycleways and bus lanes to encourage cycling and using the bus
- developing transport plans to encourage park-and-ride
- giving grants to help insulate homes/rooms, etc.
- working with schools to help educate pupils about saving energy
- using longlife bulbs in their public buildings
- making public buildings as energy efficient as possible
- encouraging its own staff to save energy by recycling, e.g. plastic cups/paper.

What is Agenda 21?

Source **D** is one local council's view of what the future is about for the people living in one part of the UK. It is based on the principles of **Agenda 21**. Agenda 21 is an idea that came out of the 1992 Rio 'Earth Summit', where leaders from around the world agreed to work towards a more sustainable future. They agreed that all local areas should produce their own local Agenda 21 plans.

STEP 2

1 Look at the article **B** about the planning decision. Why were some people objecting to the scheme?

2 Why do people get so concerned about local developments that affect them?

3 Look at photo **A**. Where are the nearest recycling bins in your area?

4 What has your local council done to improve your local area? See source **C**.

5 Look at source **D** – the list of plans for Oldham. Which do you think are the five most important?

Homework

Find out more about your own council's plans for Agenda 21. They are often found as part of the local council's web site or by contacting the planning office.

D

Oldham's Agenda 21

'You gotta have a dream, if you don't have a dream, how you gonna make a dream come true.' South Pacific, musical.

'Where there is no vision the people perish.' Proverbs 18, *The Bible*.

Oldham's Agenda 21 is a vision, in short, of a sustainable Oldham. This plan sets out this vision and is the first attempt at 'joined up thinking' for the whole borough and its people. It differs from the many other plans that exist for the borough in that it wasn't produced by experts in consultation with people, but actually by the people of Oldham through focus groups, questionnaires, art projects and visioning workshops.

Some of the actions required to make this vision a reality can be achieved instantly, others will take a little more time and effort. To achieve a more sustainable Oldham will require the involvement of all people – from businesses, the Local Authority, the Police, the Health Authority, to schools, voluntary groups and individuals – everyone has a part to play.

This document has set out the vision of the type of Oldham the people of Oldham wish to see. It has brought together different views, different cultures and age groups.

- It is for an Oldham of clean streets and decent housing.
- Where there are many green parks and where it is safe to play, walk or sit.
- An Oldham of 'green corridors', open spaces and woodland, where wildlife abounds.
- Where leisure facilities are close to hand and cheap enough for people to afford.
- A town where people of different abilities and different cultures support each other and live in harmony.
- Where our industrial past is celebrated but we live for the future.
- Where all people's opinions are asked for and acted upon and health and support services are accessible and affordable.
- Where traffic is reduced, and public transport is less expensive, safer and more reliable.
- It is where useful employment is available and unpaid work is valued and where waste, of resources and people, is reduced.

Oldham Agenda 21 Plan (adapted)

One local borough's view of the future, 'The Vision for the 21st Century'

What can governments do?

Your **Member of Parliament (MP)** represents the views of people in the local **constituency**. Members of Parliament also vote and 'sit' on committees in the Houses of Parliament which decide on whether new things are built (like roads or housing) and whether areas of land are protected or not. Do you know which constituency you live in? Do you know who your local Member of Parliament is?

The national government and Parliament has a great deal of influence on people's lives. Its decisions affect jobs, education, health, transport, industry and the environment. Laws are passed which affect what people can, and cannot, do – they can affect you!

A

Houses of Parliament

B

Government minister announcing new development

The national government also represents you at international conferences that decide on issues to do with world trade, world poverty, aid and the global environment. Different 'parties' (Labour, Conservative, Liberal Democrat and the smaller parties like the Green party) all have different 'policies' on many of these issues. Individuals can choose to vote for these parties during local and general elections. Do you know which party controls your local council?

National and local governments also try to make improvements in people's lives by reducing unemployment, crime and community tension. These problems are also affected by local circumstances. Local communities can also set up their own community groups to help solve some of these problems. Often people give up their own time to help these voluntary groups.

STEP 3

1 Are there any national government decisions that have affected life in your area recently?
2 How does the type of area you live in affect the amount of unemployment, crime and community tension? What can be done to try and overcome some of these issues?
3 Imagine you were writing to your local MP or councillor. What would be the issues that you would like to mention, complain about or thank them for?

Extension

Plot on a local street map the areas where graffiti and vandalism occur. How does the pattern of graffiti and vandalism compare to the type of housing and street pattern? Produce a plan for reducing some of these problems by using new technologies and plans, e.g. CCTV, redesign of streets and buildings, street lighting, etc.

THINKING THROUGH YOUR ENQUIRY

'A vision for the local area?'

Look at the Agenda 21 statement made by Oldham borough council on page 107 and box C on this page. What do you think your local council statement should be like?

1 In order to make suggestions to your council about what needs to be done in your local area you will need to survey the area. One group (group A) could carry out an environmental survey. Another group (group B) could produce a questionnaire and ask people their thoughts about the local area.

2 Write a formal report of your findings – called 'A vision for our local area'.

3 Compare your ideas with your plans and the local Agenda 21 document for Oldham.

4 Make a poster/presentation to show your main findings.

Group A

- Carry out an environmental survey in a part of your local area – it might be a single street or road to represent a neighbourhood or district. Identify and record the quality of the environment. Use headings such as: quality of buildings, density of buildings, noise, litter, graffiti, parking, safety, street lighting, etc.
- You might give each a score from 1 (poor) to 5 (good).
- Collect information using agreed criteria. Map and present your data using a variety of techniques – such as ICT and those suggested by your teacher.

Are there any differences in the environmental quality of your local area?

Group B

- Carry out a survey of opinions about the local area. Make up five or six questions to find out what they think about local services, shopping areas, leisure facilities, the local environment, etc.
- Ask a variety of people from different age groups and different parts of the community (if possible).
- Try and find out if there are any local action/community groups who are trying to make improvements (Steps 1 and 2).
- Record and present your data using ICT and those suggested by your teacher.

Taking into account the results of your survey and investigations, suggest three or four key actions the local council could take to improve the life of people in your local area (Step 3).

C Summary of Oldham's Agenda 21

The Oldham plan aims to improve life for people in the area. It has 21 steps, including: biodiversity, pollution, wildlife habitats, recreation, transport, energy, waste, recycling, access, information, equality, food, employment, education, democracy, poverty, health, natural resources, consumer power, access to open space, and quality of the human environment.

Extension

Send the report/presentation to your local council and ask them to respond or invite a local planner or councillor to discuss the council's Agenda 21 plans with you.

6b Tomorrow's citizens
• One world? •

- How are people around the world connected to each other?

- How do patterns of wealth vary from place to place?

- How is the world changing?

We live in a world which is changing very fast. Many of these changes mean that we rely on other people and other countries much more than we did in the past.

A

And here is the world news. World leaders met today to discuss world trade and world poverty. There were protests from angry demonstrators who don't think the world's richest countries are doing enough to help the world's poorest people.

B

C

'The Earth does not belong to man, man belongs to the Earth. All things are connected. Whatever befalls the Earth befalls the sons of the Earth. Man did not weave the web of life; he is merely a strand in it. Whatever he does to the web, he does to himself.'

Chief Seattle, Native American, 1900s

Link from MEDC supermarket to local farmer in LEDC

YOUR ENQUIRY

In this enquiry you will begin to describe and explain:

- how the world is becoming a global community
- the patterns of wealth
- the ways in which people and places are connected to each other across the world.

At the end of the enquiry you will design a web site to show to other students how these topics of interdependence and globalisation are affecting people all over the world.

How you affect people in other countries

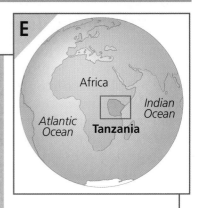

E

Africa

Atlantic Ocean

Indian Ocean

Tanzania

D Tatu Museyni, a 37-year-old African women, made less than £11 last year from the coffee she grows on her farmland in Tanzania. She is like thousands of small coffee producers all over the world. During the past twelve months the price of coffee on the world market has fallen by 50%. The same has happened to other food products such as bananas, tea, cocoa, chocolate, sugar and honey. When prices fall, small farmers hardly get enough money to survive. In order to help some of these small farmers, fairtrade organisations have been set up to try and pay farmers a fairer price for their goods. In March 2001, fairtrade organisations launched a Fairtrade Fortnight to encourage people to buy more fairtrade goods. Some supermarkets in the UK now have their own fairtrade products. The total value of fairtrade coffee is only 2% of the total market and only 1 in 20 people buy fairtrade goods. The effect of the fall in world coffee prices on the world stock markets may seem a long way from Tatu's ordinary life in Tanzania – but for her son Isaiah it will mean the difference between going to school and not going to school.

From *The Times,* 10th March, 2001

What you and your family buy can affect people in other places. Their living and working conditions can depend on whether we buy things from that country and what price we are prepared to pay for the goods. The price of things on the world market can decide whether they get enough money to do the things they want to do. What you buy can also affect the environment in other places, either directly or indirectly.

STEP 1

1 Look at the information on pages 110–11. List three ways in which you are linked with other countries around the world.

2 Explain how a change in people's choices in one country could affect the lives of people in another country like Tanzania.

3 Look at the source **D**. What happened to the price of coffee on the world markets?

4 How did this affect the life of Isaiah and her mother?

5 What can people do in this country to help people like Tatu Museyni?

6 Look at source **F**. How can people in countries like Tanzania help themselves?

F

In parts of Tanzania people are working together in cooperatives.
On the slopes of Mount Kilimanjaro, at 4,700ft, Phillip Tesha grows coffee as part of the Kilimanjaro Native Cooperative Union:

'We pay people by the amount of coffee they pick – we are all equal – we started the union in the 1950s when farmers banded together to make sure they got the right price for their coffee. We did not use insecticides and after a while our crops produced more than those that did. We were growing 'organic' coffee before it became more popular. We were approached by Cafedirect who told us they could cut out the 'middlemen' and sell our coffee direct to the supermarkets in the UK. Today I feel the future is more optimistic for us coffee growers.'

Interdependence – what does it mean?

As we have seen, what one person does in one part of the world is often connected to what other people are doing in other parts of the world. We can communicate with each other much more easily. Many people are in constant communication with friends and relatives and other people in other parts of the world. Through television and the Internet we can see pictures and talk to people in places on the other side of the world. Some people say that the world is now a **global village** and that we are all **global citizens** of the world.

In the past, communities and countries were much more **independent**. Now people all over the world rely on other people, often in other countries, to provide the things they need. We are now all connected to each other – we are all **interdependent**. What you and your family buy can affect people in other places: in the UK, Europe and overseas.

Decisions made by people in other parts of the world can also affect people in your country. If a large company based in another country decides to close a factory in the UK, large numbers of people can suddenly become unemployed and the whole of the community can suffer. On the other hand, companies in the UK can suddenly win new business in another country and create new jobs, which benefits the whole community.

Trade

Things that we need come from all over the world. Our supermarkets are full of food grown in different time zones and areas which are experiencing a different season to us. When it is winter here, it is summer there.

In order to pay for **imports** from other countries we produce goods, which we sell and **export** to other countries.

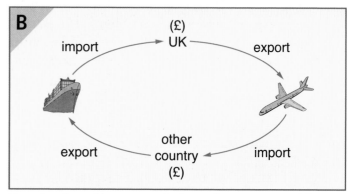

People in other countries who export things to the UK are dependent on whether or not we choose to buy their products. We also depend on people in other countries buying our exports.

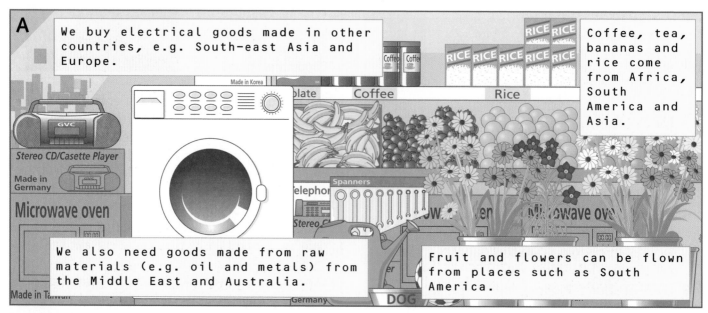

Supermarket goods from all over the world

 • citizenship – interdependence •

Globalisation – is the world getting smaller, or is everywhere the same?

A motor car could be designed in Japan, built in the UK from components which come from all over the world, transported and sold to someone in a European country.

Now we can buy goods from a different country over the Internet. These large transnational companies have tremendous influence on what we eat, what car we drive, what electrical goods we use and what we wear. Today many places seem the same with the same shops, cars, clothes and food to sell. The world's largest companies are now richer than many of the world's countries.

In the past, people's lives often changed very little from birth to death. Before the industrial revolution, technology changed very slowly. Most people worked where they lived and only travelled very short distances, perhaps occasionally to their nearest market town about five miles away. Most people grew their own food and made things for themselves. Local craftsmen made the things people needed, many of the materials, such as wood, were available locally. People's lives were more **sustainable**. Places were very different with their own distinctive types of houses, foods, clothes and lifestyle.

With the growth of trade, things began to be brought to Britain from all over the world. Gradually we came to rely more and more on things produced in other countries. More recently multinational companies began to produce things all over the world and sell them in every country. These companies are now called **transnational companies (TNCs)**. These companies have different parts of their organisation all over the world. The company's products are designed, produced, delivered and sold in different countries.

STEP 2

1 On an outline map, show how you are connected to different places around the world through friends, relatives, holidays, things that you buy and things that you watch on television.
2 How could a decision made in a transnational company's boardroom in Tokyo, Japan, affect the lives of people living in England, Scotland or Wales?
3 How has the introduction of the Internet speeded up the process of interdependence and globalisation?
4 Make a list of two positive and two negative effects of globalisation for people in this country and in a less economically developed country.
5 Imagine a conversation between two people: one from a richer, developed country and one from a poorer, less economically developed country. Draw a cartoon to show some of the comments they might make about globalisation.

• draw a cartoon •

Unequal shares?

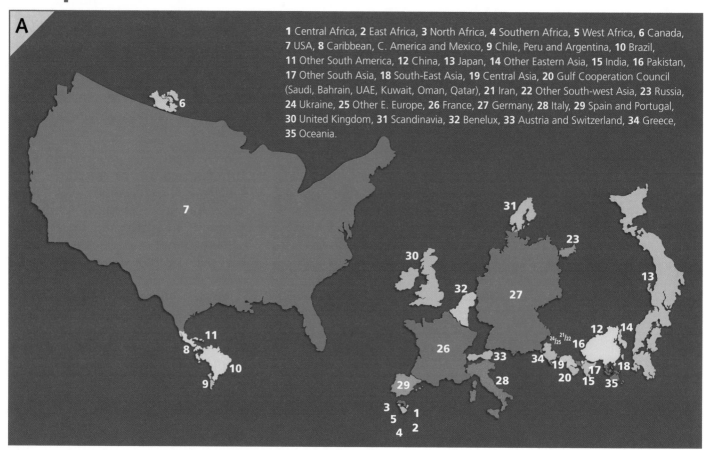

A

1 Central Africa, 2 East Africa, 3 North Africa, 4 Southern Africa, 5 West Africa, 6 Canada, 7 USA, 8 Caribbean, C. America and Mexico, 9 Chile, Peru and Argentina, 10 Brazil, 11 Other South America, 12 China, 13 Japan, 14 Other Eastern Asia, 15 India, 16 Pakistan, 17 Other South Asia, 18 South-East Asia, 19 Central Asia, 20 Gulf Cooperation Council (Saudi, Bahrain, UAE, Kuwait, Oman, Qatar), 21 Iran, 22 Other South-west Asia, 23 Russia, 24 Ukraine, 25 Other E. Europe, 26 France, 27 Germany, 28 Italy, 29 Spain and Portugal, 30 United Kingdom, 31 Scandinavia, 32 Benelux, 33 Austria and Switzerland, 34 Greece, 35 Oceania.

Topological map showing the wealth of the world's countries from *The Times millennium special*

Despite the world economy becoming global, some countries remain rich compared to others. The gap between the rich and poor countries is still vast.

B

	Difference between the richest and poorest countries in terms of exports (1996)	
	Country	Exports (Millions of US $)
Highest 5	USA	575,477
	Germany	511,728
	Japan	410,481
	France	283,318
	UK	259,039
Lowest 5	Chad	125
	Central African Republic	115
	Niger	79
	Guinea-Bissau	56
	Burundi	37

C

Campaigner at Debt Jubilee 2000 Rally

• differences in wealth development •

Debt

Many of the world's poorest countries owe money to world banks and richer countries. They borrowed money in the past to fund projects and schemes. Many of the poorest countries still have to spend one fifth of all they earn on paying off their debts. The world's richest countries have agreed to cancel many of these debts, but some groups want them to go further and cancel all the debts owed by the poorer countries.

STEP 3

1 Mark the countries named in table **B** on an outline map of the world. Describe the location of the richest and poorest countries. Are there any patterns?
2 Look at Map **A** – what type of map is this?
3 Describe the pattern of wealth shown in map **A**. Why is this a good way to show it?
4 What does photo **C** show you about unequal shares?

THINKING THROUGH YOUR ENQUIRY

'Tomorrow's citizens'

'On the world stage we are also building partnerships. Globalisation has made it necessary for all of us to take a world view. We cannot now escape the fact that we all depend on each other for our future. The role of nation states has altered in the face of globalisation. Within developing countries we will work with governments and non-governmental organisations (NGOs) to deliver basic rights and services directly to the poorest people, but our plan recognises that to achieve real progress we need to work more widely with groups of governments, through international institutions and with business. To do anything else is to ignore the way in which the world is changing. Globalisation may present new challenges for us, but we cannot pretend that it does not exist.'

Clare Short, Secretary of State
for International Development (DFID)

You task is to design a web site called 'Tomorrow's citizens' to put onto your school's intranet site or web site. It will help other pupils and students in your school understand the complex issues studied in this enquiry. This might be done as part of your school's work on global **citizenship**. This could be carried out in groups of four or five. If you have not got access to a computer, you could design the pages on paper to start with.

Page 1

Your title page should have a striking photograph or illustration and a title, e.g. 'Becoming a global citizen'.

Page 1 also needs links to four or five other pages, these could be called:
'Interdependence', 'Globalisation', 'Oneworld/ Fairtrade', 'Sustainable development', 'Global citizen' or 'The debt crisis'.

One person or a pair/small group could design each page.

Pages 2 to 6

- Using Steps 1 to 3 to help you, design individual pages on one of the topics suggested or a similar topic heading, e.g. 'How can we help?', 'What can you do?', 'Rich world – poor world', 'Global events in the news'.
- Each page will have a brief **explanation** of the term you have chosen.
- Using the textbook and web sites, choose a map, photograph, set of statistics or a graph to illustrate one or two important aspects of your topic.
- Text on each page will **explain how people are linked together** in different ways.
- If you have the time (or for homework) you could make further links (or pages) to produce small case studies, which help to explain how these issues/topics affect different people around the world (see page 111 as an example).

 • design a website • • data handling •

6c Tomorrow's citizens

• Tomorrow's world – our common future? •

- How can we protect the environment for future generations?

- What can be done at local, national and global scales?

- How can we develop a more sustainable future?

People have different views about development and the future of the environment. We are all citizens of tomorrow's world. Some people have a greater effect on the environment than others do, but we all have **rights and responsibilities** connected to the environment. Some people would say we have a right to fresh air, clean water, wholesome food and places for recreation and leisure. Although we might all agree on the basic needs, people do not agree on the best way to achieve these things. Some people think that new technology and increasing the number of things we have is the best way forward. Others think that we need a more **sustainable** way of living, that makes the most of what we have. But for many people in the world, clean water and wholesome foods are still luxuries.

Environmental poster at a West African Nature Reserve (Abuko) in the Gambia

YOUR ENQUIRY

In this enquiry you will:
- develop an understanding of the way that people affect the environment
- have the opportunity to discuss economic, political and environmental issues
- discuss the way that various groups can help protect and sustain the environment.

At the end of this enquiry you will draft a speech for the Prime Minister to give at the Rio +10 Conference [Summit] outlining four ways to prevent further damage to the environment.

What is the problem?

B

'In April 1987 the United Nations asked Norway's Prime Minster (Mrs Gro Harlem Brundtland) to write a report about how the world's rapidly growing population would meet its basic needs in the 21st Century. The Brundtland Report stated that:
"When the (20th) century began, neither people or technology had the power to affect the Earth's systems. Now, not only do the vastly increased numbers and their activities have that power, but major unintended changes have occurred in the atmosphere, in soils, in waters, among plants and animals and in the relationships among all these things." '

Our Common Future, final report of the World Commission on Environment and Development (adapted)

What can individual people, voluntary organisations, business and governments do to try and solve some of the world's environmental problems? Different people have different views on what can be done and when.

C

We will increase the percentage of energy we use from alternative sources from 2% to 10%.

Politician

Today's announcement is only words. We want action now!

Environmental group representative

It's all very confusing – who do I agree with?

Student

STEP 1

1 Can you think of one thing that you will do today which will affect the environment in some way (e.g. using energy or resources)?
2 What do you throw away eventually, what do you keep? What do you recycle?
3 Look at the views of people in **C**.
Is the protection of the environment as simple as this?
Are some people only interested in more money and owning more things?
Aren't we all keen to have a **higher standard of living** without destroying the planet?
What do you think? Discuss this with another person.
What does the class think?

Extension

What did the Brundtland Report identify as some of the key problems facing the planet in the 21st century?

What do you think is meant by 'unintended changes'?

Can you give an example of unintended changes on: the atmosphere, soils, rivers and oceans or plants and animals?

Why are there environmental problems?

A

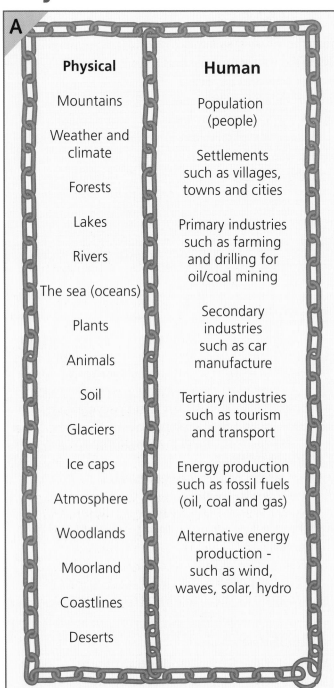

Physical	Human
Mountains	Population (people)
Weather and climate	Settlements such as villages, towns and cities
Forests	
Lakes	Primary industries such as farming and drilling for oil/coal mining
Rivers	
The sea (oceans)	
Plants	Secondary industries such as car manufacture
Animals	
Soil	Tertiary industries such as tourism and transport
Glaciers	
Ice caps	Energy production such as fossil fuels (oil, coal and gas)
Atmosphere	
Woodlands	Alternative energy production – such as wind, waves, solar, hydro
Moorland	
Coastlines	
Deserts	

The environment is interconnected

In this series of books you have studied many different aspects of the environment. You have studied aspects of the **physical** environment. You have also studied aspects of the **human** environment. Much of the physical environment has been affected by people's actions. They are both **interconnected**.

B

Pollution of the environment

C

Key questions for the future – what do you think?

- Do we understand how human activities affect the natural environment and the planet's systems, e.g. climate change and global warming?

- Why do we need to keep a balance between the physical and human environment, e.g. the numbers of people, industry and resources?

- How can the aspects of the human environment be developed in the future in a more sustainable way, e.g. use of energy, the growth of cities?

Is sustainable development the answer?

Sustainable development is 'development that meets the needs of the present without compromising the ability of future generations to meet their own needs' *Brundtland Report* 1987.

What can you do to help?

What can the individual person do to prevent further damage to the environment or protect the environment? Diagram **E** gives some examples.

D

Minister for the Environment Michael Meacher was on hand to meet the young visitors at the opening of Meanwood Valley Urban Farm's new environmental 'EpiCentre'. Meanwood in Leeds is one of 16 sites in the Soil Association's Organic Farms Network, and the EpiCentre is an imaginative and interactive venture providing education and training in the heart of the city. The building itself is an excellent working example, incorporating such elements as a turf roof, composting toilets, energy efficient heating and reed bed drainage treatment.

From *Living Earth,* Soil Association No.204, Oct–Dec 1999

EpiCentre in Leeds

E

- Use less energy – electricity or fuel (petrol) – walk more
- Switch it off?
- Wear more clothes at home – turn the heat down
- Only boil the right amount of water you need
- Take a shower not a bath
- Insulate or double glaze your home
- Don't drop litter – recycle – avoid buying disposable goods
- Write to your local council, councillor, Member of Parliament MP, MEP
- Join a voluntary environmental group (local/national)

Homework

1 Choose a different aspect of the environment and design a poster to show ways of protecting/improving the environment.
2 Research one voluntary organisation (NGO) local or global, that is trying to protect the environment, e.g. WWF, Friends of the Earth and Greenpeace (see Longman web site). Using the Internet, describe one of their current campaigns to protect the environment.

STEP 2

1 Look at the features of the physical environment in box **A** and photos **B** and **C**. Explain how human activity might damage any three aspects of the physical environment (e.g. pollution of lakes and rivers by industry dumping waste).
2 For two aspects of the physical environment, explain how people are trying to protect or improve them, either locally, nationally or internationally (e.g. organic farming to protect the soil).
3 Look at box **A**. Explain how changes to any two of these human activities could improve the human environment, e.g. cleaner transport in cities, recycling.
4 Look at source **E**. Write a diary or draw a storyboard to explain how one person could affect the environment directly or indirectly in a day.

What can industry do?

A

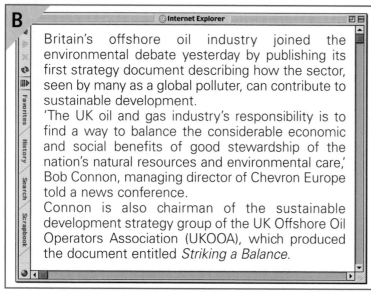

B

Britain's offshore oil industry joined the environmental debate yesterday by publishing its first strategy document describing how the sector, seen by many as a global polluter, can contribute to sustainable development.

'The UK oil and gas industry's responsibility is to find a way to balance the considerable economic and social benefits of good stewardship of the nation's natural resources and environmental care,' Bob Connon, managing director of Chevron Europe told a news conference.

Connon is also chairman of the sustainable development strategy group of the UK Offshore Oil Operators Association (UKOOA), which produced the document entitled *Striking a Balance*.

From Tidy Britain web page,
Striking a Balance, 14th August 2001

The Worldwide Fund for Nature (WWF) has encouraged businesses to adopt new ideas to reduce their contribution to global warming.

- **Denmark** WWF worked with the Danish Minister for Energy and Environment and the country's wind energy industry to produce energy from wind power.
- **Germany** WWF persuaded a company to improve the energy efficiency of their leading products by 25%. AEG agreed to sell only the most energy-efficient class of household appliances.
- **Japan** WWF organised meetings on energy efficiency, attended by major corporations.
- **The Netherlands:** WWF brought together housebuilders and energy experts to incorporate available energy-saving technologies into new homes.

STEP 3

1 Using this page and your own research, write down as many ways that you can think of where industry can help the environment. Use these headings: 'Energy', 'Transport', 'Waste and Pollution', 'Food and Agriculture', 'Water' and 'Fairtrade'.

2 Make up an advertisement for a company selling an environmentally friendly product in the future, e.g. mini windmills for individual homes. Draw a picture and explain its advantages. You could do this on a computer.

What can voluntary organisations do?

Voluntary organisations, sometimes called NGO (non-governmental organisations), can also help people and the environment in different parts of the world.

Case study

In the hot, dry Caatinga region of North-east Brazil, Joao Pedro's land was so dry that the soil ran through his fingers like sand. Now he grows enough fruit and vegetables to feed his family. How did he do it?

The problem

- For much of the year there is not enough rainfall, hardly any rain at all in 1998.
- Normal water supplies have dried up.
- Families don't have any food and rely on money from the government.
- The land has been 'overused' and is now exhausted of goodness in the soil.

What can be done?

- Oxfam supports a farming training centre called 'Caatinga'.
- Technicians from the centre help farmers build dams and show them ways of collecting and storing water.
- The centre provides loans to help farmers build their own dams.
- Other farmers come to see what Joao Pedro has done.

'Before I built the dam, all the land was poor and crops would not grow well. Now my fields are green with trees, beans, papaya and other crops. My family won't go hungry again.'

The project may just make the difference to farmers who are struggling to survive and prevent them moving to cities to look for work.

C

Help them build a future free from hunger and disease

PHOTO: Jenny Matthews/OXFAM

...for just £2 a month

Oxfam

ENVIRONMENTALLY FRIENDLY PAPER

Oxfam advert

STEP 4

1 Look at the information on this page. In small groups, produce a short script and directions for a brief five-minute video about the work of Oxfam in the Caatinga region of Brazil. You might include an introduction by the presenter, interviews with people involved and information in the form of maps or graphics.

or

Research what one of the following organisations is doing to help people and protect the environment (use the Internet):
OXFAM   Action Aid   Christian Aid
CAFOD   UNICEF
Give a short presentation on the work of one of these organisations or produce a script for a short video (as above).

What can governments and international organisations do?

Governments from around the world agreed the 'Kyoto Protocol' in December 1997. This was to try and control the emissions of greenhouse gases, particularly carbon dioxide, to prevent global warming.

A

What is the European Union doing?

The EU has committed itself to cut greenhouse gas emissions by 8% between 2008 and 2012 when it signed the Kyoto Protocol. This will require a shift to sustainable renewable energy sources, including solar as well as super efficient buildings, appliances and cars.

Since the Brundtland report in 1987 there have been a number of government plans, international meetings and organisations set up to try and do something about environmental and development issues around the world. Many of these groups do not affect the environment directly, but their decisions affect the way people live and use the environment. The conferences do not always go smoothly. Sources **B** and **C** are from a WWF report on two conferences.

B

Climate Summit, November 2000

Governments agreed on legally-binding emission reduction targets in Kyoto back in 1997. But the rich nations missed a golden opportunity in November 2000 to make a break with their polluting past.

The United States, Japan, Canada and Australia brought November's talks to a halt. They insisted on exploiting loopholes in the Kyoto agreement that would have allowed them to avoid cutting their global warming pollution while still claiming to be meeting their Kyoto targets. This proved too much for the countries from the European Union to accept.

WWF Report

C

Climate Summit, July 2001

In January and February 2001, governments from around the world approved a new global agreement on the science, impacts and solutions to global warming. The situation is crying out for urgent action by industrialised nations to reduce their carbon dioxide emissions. Time's running out for making the Kyoto climate treaty and for cuts in global warming pollution that have to be made in the coming decades.

The main areas of disagreement are:

- whether industrialised countries could claim credit for carbon dioxide control projects set up in developing countries
- the extent to which priority is given to preventing carbon dioxide emissions, rather than planting trees to try and temporarily soak up carbon dioxide from the atmosphere.

WWF Report

STEP 4

1 Why is it important that countries from around the world agree to cut greenhouse gas emissions?

2 What can individuals do to try and influence these national and international organisations?

3 Imagine you were writing to your local MP or national government before one of these major international conferences. Write a persuasive letter explaining your concerns about the environment and suggest one way that international organisations might help to improve the environment.

Why geographers make good citizens!

In Book 1 you were asked the question 'What is Geography?'. Hopefully you could now answer that question if someone asked you and also see why *geographers make good citizens*.

Geographers:

- learn about things which are important to people's lives, like jobs and the environment

- begin to understand how people's actions affect the world around us

- explain the reasons why things are the way they are

- can communicate information in maps, diagrams, photographs and write reports about important issues

- play a part in discussing issues

- can take action – by joining or contributing to a voluntary group.

THINKING THROUGH YOUR ENQUIRY

'Rio +10 World Summit'

The Rio Earth Summit was a conference which took place in Rio de Janeiro where the world's leaders got together to try and find some solutions to the problems facing the world's people and the environment. Another conference is due to take place to review the progress made since the last conference. It will be called Rio plus 10 (10 years later): 'Rio +10 World Summit'.

You are asked to draft a speech for the Prime Minister for the Rio +10 World Summit, or the next major world environmental conference. The speech will be about ways to prevent further environmental damage to the planet. You need to come up with four ways that we can either prevent further damage or help to improve the environment. You have decided to give five examples in the speech, as follows.

- **Example 1:**
  One way in which *individuals* can help prevent further damage or help improve the environment (see Unit 6a, and Steps 1 and 2).

- **Example 2:**
  One way that a *community* (like a school, village or urban area) can help prevent further damage or help improve the environment (Unit 6a).

- **Example 3:**
  One way that *industry* could help prevent further damage or help improve the environment (Step 3).

- **Example 4:**
  One way that *national governments* could help prevent further damage or help improve the environment (e.g. passing laws).

- **Example 5:**
  One way that *international governmental groups* or *non-governmental organisations* (NGOs) could prevent further damage to the environment (Step 4).

Draft the speech (it could be in note form).

You might like to give some facts and figures, but try to capture people's imagination and interest.

Try to include either ideas from the whole of Unit 6, or your own ideas, or an example from your own local area/research.

Why not take action – send it to the Prime Minister!

Glossary

Active volcano — Volcano which has erupted recently

Aftershocks — Smaller shocks occurring in an area after a very large earthquake

Agenda 21 — Local plans for sustainable development

Amenities — Facilities provided for people, e.g. library, leisure centre, parks

Berth (port) — Individual part of a quay where ships moor

Brownfield site — Area of land that has been built upon and now is derelict

Canyon — Very deep (often steep-sided) gorge or ravine – often used instead of 'gorge' in the USA

Caribou — Type of deer found in the Arctic regions of North America

Citizens — People who live in a place and are allowed to vote

Colliery — Coal mine

Commuters — People who travel to another place to work every day

Composite volcano — Volcano made up of layers of lava and ash

Cone (volcanic) — The shape of many volcanoes with the crater at the centre

Confluence — Place where two rivers meet

Conservative plate boundary — Where the plates of the Earth are sliding past one another

Conserve — Make something (e.g. non-renewable resource) last for a long time

Constituency — Area of the country represented by an MP (Member of Parliament)

Constructive plate boundary — Where two plates of the Earth move apart and new crust is forming, (e.g. in the mid Atlantic)

Container terminal — Part of a port, road or rail network that handles containers

Country park — Smaller areas of land, often close to towns and cities for recreation and conservation, usually managed by the local council

Convection current — Movement of heat – in the Earth's crust, molten rock rises towards the surface and drops down as it is cooled, this causes circular convection

Councillor — Person who represents an area and decides how to provide for the local people

County Councillor — Person who helps to decide what is done in a county

Crust — Surface layer of the Earth, it can be up to 40 km deep

Deforest — Widespread cutting down of trees

Destructive plate boundary — Where two plates come together and crust is slowly destroyed

Dormant (volcano) — A sleeping volcano, one that has not erupted for a very long time

Earthquake — Vibrations of the Earth's crust caused by movements along fault lines

Economic — Connected with jobs, trade, industry and services

Economic miracle — Very rapid economic growth which brings wealth to a country

Economic structure — The number, type and distribution of industry within a country

Epicentre — Position on the surface of the Earth directly above the focus of an earthquake

Eruption (volcanic) — When materials such as lava and volcanic bombs are emitted from a volcano

Export — Goods sold to other countries

Extinct (volcano) — Dead volcano, one that is no longer active

Evolved — Slow change in character over time of plants and animals as they become better adapted to their environment

Factory retail outlet — Shopping centre which sells factory seconds and end-of-line items

Fail safe — Safety systems that are put in place to stop damaging events happening

Far East — Collective name for the countries of south-east Asia

Favela — Brazilian word for shanty town

Fault lines — Lines of weakness in the Earth's crust

Focus — The place in the Earth's crust where an earthquake originates

Global citizens — Idea that we all belong to one world

Globalisation — The spread of industries around the world

Global village — Idea that the world is 'getting smaller' due to better communications

Global warming — Heating up of the atmosphere

Granite — Hard, crystalline igneous rock

Greenfield site — Site for building, previously farmland or countryside

Greenwich Meridian — The zero degrees line of longitude which passes through Greenwich in London – the line on which time around the world is based

Hanging valley	Smaller side valley in glacial areas – its floor hangs high above the floor of the major valley that it joins
Hectare	Area of land 100 metres by 100 metres square
Hot spot (crustal)	Weakness in the Earth's crust through which molten rock can punch its way towards the surface
Human	To do with people, settlement, transport, factories etc
Impact	Effect of something happening.
Import	Goods bought from other countries
Incandescent	Bright light caused by high temperature of material such as lava
Industrial estate	Purpose-built industrial units in a specific area
Infant mortality rate	Number of children who die in the first year of life (per thousand population)
Inflation	When prices increase
Infra-structure	The main structure of an organisation, e.g. the key roads and railways of a region or country
Inner city	Area surrounding the city centre
Interconnected	Things and people that affect each other because they are linked together
Interdependent	Idea that people and places rely on each other
Irrigate	To water the land artificially
Latitude	Degrees north or south of the Equator
LEDC	Less economically developed country
Life expectancy	Age that people can be expected to live to
Living standards	People's wages
Local council	People who run local services and decide what to do locally
Longitude	Degrees east or west of the Greenwich Meridian
Magnitude	The strength of events such as earthquakes
Mantle (Earth)	The part of the Earth between the crust and the outer core
Manufacturing	Making or producing goods
Market place	Where goods are sold to customers
MEDC	More economically developed country
Member of Parliament (MP)	Person who represents an area of the country

Migration	Movement of people from one place to another
Molten	Molten rock in the mantle of the Earth is in a semi-liquid or molten state
National Park	Large protected area of natural beauty
Native American	First people to inhabit North America
Natural increase	Population increase resulting from higher birth rate than death rate
Nautical mile	Unit of distance used on water, equal to 1853 metres
National debt	Amount of money a country owes
NIC	Newly industrialising country
Non-renewable (resources)	Resources that cannot be replaced, e.g. coal, oil
Nuee ardente	Large cloud of ash or dust that often hangs over a volcano
Outworkers	Self-employed people who do work for a company
Overpopulated	Too many people compared to the resources available
Pack ice	Large area of floating ice near the poles of the Earth
Permafrost	Parts of the soil or ground below the surface that are frozen solid all year
Physical	Natural features, e.g. rivers, hills, weather, forests, oceans
Physical structure	Soil, vegetation, climate and physical features of a country
Piece rate	Rate of pay by the number of items made
Population density	Number of people per kilometre squared
Population density	Number of people per square mile
Population distribution	Spread of people across an area
Primary (earthquake) impacts	The immediate impact of earthquakes, such as the tremors and destruction of buildings
Public enquiry	Meeting at which members of the public or groups can put their points of view about proposed developments
Pyroclastic	Extremely hot pieces of ash and dust emitted from volcanoes
Quality of living	How happy people are with their life
Reclaimed land	Land that has been recovered from water or from other uses for re-use
Recover	When plants grow back over time

Glossary

Redevelop	To knock down and rebuild
Reef	Rocks (often coral) close to the sea surface – a danger to shipping
Regional disparities	Differences that exist between areas
Regional economy	The buying and selling of goods and the profits made in a small region of a country
Relocation	To move elsewhere
Richter scale	Scale of damage caused by earthquake action
Rights and responsibilities	What we are allowed to do and what we should do
Roches moutonnees	Very large rocks smoothed by glacial erosion on one side and more rugged on the other
Rural	Relating to the countryside
Rural depopulation	Movement of people away from the countryside
Rural-to-urban migration	To move from the countryside to towns
Seaway	Sea lane or designated route for ships when at sea
Secondary (earthquake) impacts	'After' impacts of earthquakes, e.g. the search for bodies and rebuilding of homes
Seismologist	Person who studies earthquakes and crustal movements
Sequoias	Very large type of coniferous tree found in North America
Shanty town	Poor quality housing
Shield volcano	Volcano formed of very liquid lava which flows over large distances – these cones have large diameters
Shock waves	Waves running through the Earth's crust from the focus of earthquakes
Social structure	How the population is made up, i.e. the percentage of males and females in each age group
Sound	Channel of water, often narrow, that links larger areas of water
Strato volcano	Volcano formed of layers of lava and ash
Sub-continent	Very large area of land that is a unique part of a continent, e.g. India is a unique area of the Asian continent
Sustain	To keep something going into the future at present levels
Sustainable	Resources which can be replaced or used without destroying the environment

Tariff	Tax which is put onto an import to increase its price
Textile industry	The making of cloth
Trade deficit	When a country imports more than it exports
Transnational companies	Very large companies which operate all over the world
Tundra	Vast treeless areas of the world lying close to the polar regions, characterised by having permanently frozen ground
Underpopulated	Relatively few people compared to the resources available
Urban	Built-up areas, as in towns and cities
Volcanic bomb	Large, often super-hot, boulders thrown out of volcanoes
World Heritage Site	Area of the world that is so unique that it is specially preserved by international law

Acknowledgements

We are grateful to the following for permission to reproduce
photographs and other copyright material:

Ace Photo Agency pages 73 centre (Mark Stevenson), 108 above
(Geoff Johnson); Adams Picture Library/D H Richards page 92 below
right; Aerofilms page 64; Carlos Reyes-Manzo/Andes Press Agency
page 38 left; Art Directors & TRIP pages 12 left (P Kwan), 24 right
(H Rogers), 41 (Eric Smith), 42 below (H Rogers), 79 above right, 89
above (R Belbin), 89 above centre (T Lester); Associated British Ports
Southampton pages 66, 67; Associated Press pages 44 left (Enric
Marti), 47 right (Saurabh Das); 61; PA Photos page,Camera Press
pages 62 below left (Rosenquist/Earth Images), 62 above right;
Corbis page 63; Sue Cunningham/SCP page 92 above; Daily
Telegraph 26.1.01 page 82 below right; Greg Evans International
page 94 below left; Robert Harding.com pages 19 (Simon Harris), 40
(Ken Gillham), 78 (Dr A C Waltham), 80 (Dr A C Waltham), 99 left
(Rob Cousins), 99 right; Hulton Archive pages 13 below (George
Eastman House/Lewis W Hine), 84; Hutchison Picture Library pages
10 (Melanie Friend), 22 (Victoria Ivleva), 23 (Victoria Ivleva), 30
above (Sarah Errington), 79 above left; Impact Photos pages 12 right
(John Cole), 73 below right (Thierry Bouzac); Katz Pictures/Andrew
Moore page 113; Magnum Photos page 76 below left (Paul Fusco);
Mission India/Reuters/Jason Reed page 48; News Team International
page 104; Oxfam Publishing page 121; PA Photos pages 39 below
(Rebecca Naden), 56 (EPA), 108 below, 114 (EPA); Panos Pictures
pages 20 (Marcus Rose), 33 (Chris Stowers), 42 above (Trygve
Bolstad), 85 below left (Sean Sprague), 118 above (Sanjay Acharya);
Popperfoto pages 4 right, 6 above, 44 right, 62 below right, 89 below
centre; Popperfoto/Reuters pages 13 above, 46, 47 left, 58, 82 left, 82
above right; Rex Features pages 62 above left (Fotolandia/Prisma), 62
centre right (Yves Dreton), 89 below, 94 above left, 106; Russell Sach
page 105; Science Photo Library pages 51 (Georg Gerster), 57 (E.R
Degginger), 79 below (Dr Morley Read); Seaco Picture Library page
65 above; Skyscan Photolibrary/Quick PhotoAir page 28; Soil
Association/Rupert Aker page 119; South American Pictures/Tony
Morrison pages 92 below left, 94 above centre; Still Pictures pages 21
(Tim Hjalte), 24 left (Max Milligan), 25 (Dylan Garcia), 30 below (Ron
Giling), 38 right (David Woodfall), 39 above (Max Milligan), 81 (Al
Grillo), 85 above left (John Maier), 85 above right (Mark Edwards), 94
above right (Michael Balick), 94 centre (Mark Edwards), 94 below
right (Paul Harrison), 102 (Mark Edwards), 111 (Adrian Arbib), 118
below (Jean-Leo Dugast); Topham Picturepoint pages 4 left, 5 above,
60, 85 below right.

Cover images: Tony Stone; National Geographic

We are grateful to the rights holders whose copyright material
appears in this publication.

PEARSON EDUCATION LIMITED
Edinburgh Gate, Harlow, Essex, CM20 2JE, England
and Associated companies throughout the World.

First published 2002

© Pearson Education Limited 2002

The rights of Mike Hillary, Julie Mickleburgh and Jeff Stanfield
to be identified as the authors of this Work have been asserted
by them in accordance with the Copyright, Designs and
Patents Act of 1988.

Designed, edited and produced by Gecko Ltd, Cambridge

Printed in Great Britain by Scotprint, Haddington

ISBN 0 582 400899